NON-PROFIT LEGENDS

"Hank Moore is a thought leader. Cognizant of ntributions to our world and way of life. Well researched and experienced, Legends reflects Hank's the past, he weaves the accomplishments of others into dynamic strategies. I've worked with him and admire his writings."

—**George P. Mitchell**, Chairman of Mitchell Energy & Development. Developer of The Woodlands and downtown renovation in Galveston

"Hank Moore truly embodies the concept of the Renaissance Man, from his worldly connections and involvement to his almost eerie sense of business acumen, in forecasting trends and patterns of commerce. To those of us who deal in the often delicate balance of customer and company, it is blessing to have, in Hank Moore, a resource we can depend on for fair, statesmanlike and balanced observation. I count him as a valued business friend."

—**Dan Parsons,** President, Better Business Bureau

"Every book that Hank Moore writes is a keeper. That's because of his thought leadership and ability to target what is paramount. The Legends series is not only required reading, it is blessed reading for those of us who are citizens of the world. Hank Moore brings out the grits and guts of these pioneers like nobody else could. You will be recommending these books to your friends."

—**Anthony Pizzitola**, MBA, CFM, CBCP, MBCI, Quality Assurance Manager—Jones Lang LaSalle

"I am pleased to endorse the great book, Non-Profit Legends. People like Hank Moore and the legends he writes about are what continue to make our nation better and greater. Continue your great community service for many more years. Your friend always."

—**Felix Fraga**, Neighborhood Centers, Inc. Former member of the Houston City Council. Former member of the HISD school board.

"The growth of society was fueled by opportunity, entrepreneurial spirit and commitment to community building. Hank Moore's Legends books skillfully detail the collective contributions of many great families and citizens. I'm so glad that such an important historical perspective has been written and congratulate Hank for this mighty undertaking."

—**Judson Robinson III**, President and CEO, Houston Area Urban League. Former member of the Houston City Council.

"Hank Moore is an outstanding professional, mentor, teacher, colleague and leader. He has given back to the community throughout the years to organizations and non-profits where his passion for their work is his focus. I have appreciate about him is his humbleness which counters his remarkable career and professional skills. He takes the time to talk or show up when you need him. Hank's achievements are plentiful but more importantly it is about who he is as a human being that endears him to the community. All the volunteer work he has contributed is making the world a better place in which to live."

—**Linda Toyota**, President Asian Chamber of Commerce

"Hank Moore knows more people than a person who just got elected as President of the United States, and more importantly he knows how to bring out their traits. I don't know how he does it."

—**George W. Strake Jr.**, Chairman-President of Strake Energy, Inc.

"Great cities draw upon rich histories and visionary people. I've read Hank Moore's previous books and attest that his approach to history, pop culture and business is world-class. Hank has long been a friend and trusted adviser."

—**Lee P. Brown**, Mayor of Houston, 1998-2004. Former chief of police in Houston, Atlanta and New York City.

"Hank Moore works miracles in changing stuck mindsets. He empowers knowledge from without by enthusing executives to reach within."

—**Dino Nicandros**, Chairman of the Board, Conoco

"Mr. Moore is one of the true authority figures for business and organization life. He is the only one with an Ethics Statement, which CEOs understand and appreciate."

—**Ben Love**, Vice Chairman, Chase Bank

"Hank Moore's Business Tree™ is the most original business model of the last 50 years."

—**Peter Drucker**, business visionary

"Always ahead of the trends, Hank Moore's insights are deep, applicable beyond the obvious."

—**Lady Bird Johnson**, former First Lady of the United States

"Hank Moore provides fresh approaches to heavily complex issues. His step-by-step study of the business layers makes sense. It shows how much success one could miss by trying to take shortcuts. There cannot be a price put on that kind of expertise."

—**Roy Disney**

"How can one person with so much insight into cultural history and nostalgia be such a visionary of business and organizations? Hank Moore is one of the few who understands the connection."

—**Dick Clark**, TV icon

"Hank Moore is a million dollar idea person. He is one of the few business experts whose work directly impacts a company's book value."

—**Peter Bijur,** Chairman of the Board, Texaco

"30 minutes with Hank Moore is like 30 months with almost any other brilliant business guru. He's exceptional, unlike any other, and with a testimonial list to prove it. As a speaker, he's utterly content rich, no fluff, no 'feely-touchy' nonsense, right to the point and unashamed to tell the truth. There is nobody better. Every CEO needs him."

—**Michael Hick**, Director, Global Business Initiatives

"I could not have wished for a better boss and mentor in my first professional job than Hank Moore. He leads by example, and taught me valuable lessons not only about business, but also professionalism and ethics that have stood me well throughout my career. Indeed, when I was in a position to mentor others, I've often repeated "Hank Moore stories" to my staff, and they've all heard of my first boss. Over time, I grew to understand more and more that Hank Moore treats others with respect, and thereby commands respect. I was privileged to be trained by this creative and brilliant thinker who gets more accomplished in a day than most do in a week."

—**Heather Covault**, Media Relations Manager, Writer, Web Editor at Kolo, Koloist.com

"Hank Moore brings alive the tales of these import ant individuals in a rich and detailed way that affords us all the opportunity to appreciate their co personal relationships with those legends shaping the past, present, and future. Legends is a must read."

—**Nathan Ives**, Strategy Driven.com

"Hank Moore has a wealth of knowledge. Not only is he fascinating to talk with, he's a fabulous writer as well. I'm so glad that he put all of his extensive knowledge of pop culture and business history down in a book for generations to come. Now we can all have access to the amazing stories behind many of the histories, corporations and who's who. Thanks Hank for sharing these wonderful stories. You Rock."

—**Kathryn C. Wheat**, author of the book *Networking: Naked and Unafraid*

Support and endorsement dedications: Annenberg Foundation, Baker Hughes Foundation, Carnegie Foundation, Carter Center, Disney Foundation, Duke Foundation, Ford Foundation, Gates Foundation, Kellogg Foundation, LBJ Presidential Library, Paley Foundation, Rockefeller Foundation, Swanee Hunt Foundation, United Way Worldwide, Vanderbilt Foundation, on behalf of education, learning, diversity, wisdom, community and cultural enrichment.

NON-PROFIT
LEGENDS

For Humanity & Good Citizenship

Comprehensive Reference on
Community Service, Volunteerism,
Non-Profits and Leadership

HANK MOORE

New York

NON-PROFIT LEGENDS
For Humanity & Good Citizenship
Comprehensive Reference on Community Service, Volunteerism, Non-Profits and Leadership

© 2017 HANK MOORE

Published in New York, New York, by Morgan James Publishing. Morgan James and The Entrepreneurial Publisher are trademarks of Morgan James, LLC. www.MorganJamesPublishing.com

The Morgan James Speakers Group can bring authors to your live event. For more information or to book an event visit The Morgan James Speakers Group at www.TheMorganJamesSpeakersGroup.com.

Shelfie

A **free** eBook edition is available with the purchase of this print book.

CLEARLY PRINT YOUR NAME ABOVE IN UPPER CASE

Instructions to claim your free eBook edition:
1. Download the Shelfie app for Android or iOS
2. Write your name in **UPPER CASE** above
3. Use the Shelfie app to submit a photo
4. Download your eBook to any device

ISBN 978-1-68350-158-9 paperback
ISBN 978-1-68350-159-6 eBook
ISBN 978-1-68350-160-2 hardcover
Library of Congress Control Number:
2016911417

Cover Design by:
Rachel Lopez
www.r2cdesign.com

Interior Design by:
Bonnie Bushman
The Whole Caboodle Graphic Design

In an effort to support local communities, raise awareness and funds, Morgan James Publishing donates a percentage of all book sales for the life of each book to Habitat for Humanity Peninsula and Greater Williamsburg.

Get involved today! Visit
www.MorganJamesBuilds.com

Dedicated to Joan Wilhelm.

TABLE OF CONTENTS

ACKNOWLEDGEMENTS

Acknowledgements to some of the legends whom I knew and worked with in non-profit, public sector and association service: Paula Arnold, Anna Babin, James Baker, H.E. Madame Sabine Balve, Jane Bavineau, Betty Beene, Joe Biden, Bruce Bilger, Angela Blanchard, Patty Block, Dr. Joyce Boatright, Minnette Boesel, Dr. J. Don Boney, Dr. Lee P. Brown, N. Wayne Bryant, Margie Buentello, Harold Burson, George & Barbara Bush, Neil & Maria Bush, Sarah Cartsonas, James Earl Carter, Dr. John Carver, Winston Churchill, Susan Coates, Ernie Cockrell, John & Nellie Connally, Dr. Denton Cooley, Stephen Covey, Philip B. Crosby, Robin Marcus Dahms, Price Daniel, Dr. Michael Debakey, Suzan Deison, W. Edwards Deming, Lloyd Doggett, Sharon Dotson, Peter Drucker, Dwight D. Eisenhower, Ed Emmett, Alan Erwin, Kay Fitzsimons, Gerald & Betty Ford, Brian Gallagher, Bill & Melinda Gates, Nick George, Mary Gibbs, John Glenn, Christina Goebel, Billy Graham, Dr. Norman Hackerman, Anthony Hall, David Hansen, Paula Harvey, Robert W. Harvey, Dr. Bobbie Henderson, Alvin L. Henry, Blake Hillegeist, Ann Hodge, Jack Hodson, Dr. Phillip Hoffman, Fred Hofheinz, Oveta Culp Hobby, Derrill Holly, Dr. June S. Holly, Ima Hogg, Michael Holthouse, Malcolm Host, Karen Hutchinson, Lisa Jakel, Lady Bird Johnson, Lyndon B. Johnson, Barbara Jordan, Ethel Kennedy, Joan Kennedy,

David Key, Pat Kiley, Dr. Dominique Kliger, Dr. Stephen Klineberg, Reverend William Lawson, Mickey Leland, Carl Levin, Joseph Liebermann, Ben Love, Carole Marcantel, Thurgood Marshall, Leslie Martone, Harris & Carroll Masterson, Garry Mauro, Colleen McCauley, Don McCoy, Gail J. McGovern, George & Cynthia Mitchell, Fiona Morgan, Catherine Mosbacher, Bill Moyers, Stuart & Hanni Orton, Joel Osteen, Sunshine Janda Overkamp, Dr. Rod Paige, Annise Parker, Laurence Payne, Leila Perrin, Tom Peters, Colin Powell, Patricia Smith Prather, Dr. Harry Ransom, Dr. Billy Reagan, Ronald Reagan, David Regenbaum, Ann Richards, Dr. Robert Robbins, Judson Jackie Martin, Robinson III, Carter Rochelle, Eleanor Roosevelt, Sherman Ross, Darrell Royal, Terri Royer, Frank Rynd, Jordan Rzad, Neeta Sane, Ann Schneider, John Sharp, Allan Shivers, Lisa Trapani Shumate, Preston Smith, Carole Keaton Rylander Strayhorn, Barbara Thomason, Val Thompson, Eleanor Tinsley, Harry Truman, Sylvester Turner, Candace Twyman, Jack Valenti, Mike Vance, Jose Villarreal, Cameron Waldner, Craig Washington, Shirley Weingarten, Laura Welch, Neva West, Bill White, Mark White, Kathy Whitmire, Dr. Martha Wong, Gus & Lyndall Wortham, Lee Wunsch.

Also, acknowledgements to Imad Abdullah, Sharon Connally Ammann, Tom Arbuckle, Jesse Bailey, Jim Bardwell, Robert Battle, Ann Dunphy Becker, Betty Bezemer, Judy Blake, Debra Schindler Boultinghouse, Tom Britton, Steve Brock, Sarah Buffington, Crissy Butts, Cary Carbonaro, Tony Castiglie, Glenn Chisman, Sandra Collins, George Connelly, Mike Contello, Rob Cook, John Cruise, Tom Cunningham, Hector & Arleigh De Leon, Jenna & Michael Devers, Louise Dewey, Sequoia Di Angelo, R.J. Diamond, Kallen Diggs, Sue Ditsch, Deborah Duncan, Kimberly N. Evans, Dr. Ron Evans, Chuck Finnell, Mike Flory, Felix Fraga, Yomi Garnett, Amy Gasca, Martin Gaston, Douglas Gehrman, Andrea Gold, Sonia Guimbellot, Bob Hale, John Harris, Phillip Hatfield, Royce Heslep, Michael Hick, Mary Higginbotham, Ken Hoffman, Derrill Holly, Susan & Bob Hutsko, Nathan Ives, Hiett Ives, Libby John, Chris Kelso, Dana Kervin, Soulat Khan, Jon King, Ken Klingensmith, John Kopriva, Dan Krohn, Carolyn Charlton Lamb, Kirby Lammers, Nancy Lauterbach, Sandy Lawrence, Catherine A. Le, Torre Lee, Wea Lee, Steve & Barbara Levine, Mike Linares, Craig & Vicki Loper, Jackie Lyles, Hon. Tammy Collins Markee

RCC, Ken Marsh, Aymeric Martinola, Wayne Mausbach, Brandi McDonald, Bertrand McHenry, Kathleen McKeague, Bruce Merrin, Eugene Mikle, Mark Montgomery, Julie Moore, Larry Moore, Phil Morabito, Laura Morales, Bill Nash, Tony Noun, Howard Partridge, Dan Parsons, Vaughn & Alisa Pederson, Monte Pendleton, Tom Perrone, Sue Pistone, Anthony Pizzitola, Travis Posey, Jack Pyle, Doug Quinn, Sally Mathis Ramsay, Roy & Gail Randolph, Lynn Pugh Remadna, Ronney Reynolds, Karmen Rouhana, Dr. Elizabeth Rochefort, Tamra Battle Rogers, Donna Rooney, Mike Rosen, Rob Rowland, Tony Rubleski, Christi Ruiz, Monica Ryan, Rita Santamaria, Rick Schissler, Jack Shabot, John Solis, Pravin Sonthalia, Al Spinks, Bill Spitz, Maggie Steber, Rod Steinbrook, Kaleb Steinhauer, Gail Stolzenburg, George Strake, Deanna Sullivan, Jane Moore Taylor, Charlie & Laura Thorp, Rich Tiller, James & Carolyn Todd, Linda Toyota, Carla Costa Upchurch, Kathryn van der Pol, Les Venmore, Jack Warkenthien, Louie Werderich, Kathryn C. Wheat, Rodney White, Robert Willeby, Chanel Williams, Melissa Williams, Ronald Earl Wilsher, Kyle Wilson, R.D. Yoder, Tom Ziglar.

Chapter 1

REASONS FOR CARING, GIVING AND SERVING OTHERS

I have written several books, on business, entertainment, history and pop culture. This is the one that I have been destined to write, and it has been decades in the making.

I got into volunteering and community service at an early age. I found it heartening to be a good citizen and that community stewardship made me a better professional.

I have worked with more than 1,500 non-profit, public sector, and non-governmental entities over many decades. I interfaced with many on behalf of corporate clients. I conducted independent performance reviews of many. I served on boards of directors, search committees, awards panels, review boards and task forces for many. I have spoken at conferences, strategic planning retreats, symposia, workshops and board meetings for hundreds.

Non-profit organizations are the backbone of modern society. Every individual and business should support one or many. All of us are recipients of their services, community goodwill and worthwhile objectives.

There has never been a full-scope book on non-profit service. There have been books on fundraising and some articles on volunteer management and the business aspects of running non-profit organizations.

This book covers everything non-profit, including such topics that have never appeared in an internationally published edition, such as:

- Public service announcements.
- Categories of non-profit organizations (my own creation).
- The history of volunteering and community service, spanning 300 years. This parallels a chapter in my previous book, "Pop Icons and Business Legends," where I covered a 400-year history of business.
- Strategic planning, how-to instructions.
- Pop culture influences of non-profit icons, events and campaigns.
- Communications programs for NPOs.
- Quotes on community stewardship, leadership and related topics.
- Understanding your true service.

Speaking at conferences and board retreats, I was frequently asked for a comprehensive book applicable to all the nuances of non-profit involvement. Here is what I wish to inspire via this book:

- Motivate NPOs to be unique, true to purpose and make differences.
- Encourage dialog on a Big Picture approach to non-profits.
- Inspire new dimensions to corporate philanthropy.
- Amplify discussions on community standards and ethics.
- Encourage greater collaboration and partnerships.
- Inspire a non-profit awards recognition program.
- Inspire more non-profit presence on the internet.
- Inspire more young people into community service.
- Enlighten international audiences on Western world philanthropic tenets.

Heart and Soul Reasons for Humanitarian Service

- Being good citizens.
- Volunteering, as time permits and worthy causes appear.
- Helping others.
- Business supporting communities.
- Non-profit organizations operating more business-like.
- Finding and nurturing one's passion.
- Working together with others.
- Exemplifying ethical behavior.
- Potlache: feeling happy and rewarded when serving others is appreciated.
- Sharing talents and skills.
- Innovating programs, strategies and methodologies.
- Recognizing and celebrating service.
- Honoring our elders.
- Involving young people in the lifelong quest toward community service.
- Diversity of society is reflected in service.
- Building communities.
- Interfacing with others.
- Learning from history.
- Enlightening others.
- Inspiring the next generation.
- Creating new constituencies.
- Re-involving those who have given, volunteered and participated in the past.
- Understanding the relationship of causes to quality of life.
- It's good for business, and it's the right thing to do.
- Community events are fun and entertaining.
- Knowledge is transferable from community service to family and business.
- Injects heart and soul into yourself and your stakeholders.

- Leaders exemplify legendary behavior.
- Serving the under-served.
- Predicting new community needs.
- Benefiting humanity.
- Fostering respect.
- Communicating and developing people skills.
- Being productive and fulfilled.
- Planning for future programs and community service.
- Accountability of non-profit organizations and their programs.
- Learning from failure and success.
- Putting ourselves in others' shoes.
- Visioning the future of communities and the population.
- Feeding, clothing, sheltering, educating and inspiring the needy.
- Sharing the wealth.
- Advocating for others.
- Learning more about life.
- Understanding conditions and circumstances.
- Discovering new frontiers, with opportunities to master.
- Networking, beneficial for all concerned.
- Growing as human beings and growing as a society.
- Having fun while serving.
- Humanity as the basis for global peace and understanding.

Chapter 2

THE HISTORY OF VOLUNTEERING AND COMMUNITY SERVICE

It has always been part of human nature to help others in need. Colonists banded together to survive the new nation, forming support groups to help each other plant crops, build houses and fight disease. Citizens helped neighbors to bring in harvests, build homes for the aged, maintain roads and raise barns.

Early formal institutions of volunteering were the monastic orders of churches. Monastic orders had as their mission to go into needy communities and serve. Franciscans worked with lepers, who were shunned by all others. During outbreaks of plague during the Middle Ages, it was the Franciscan monks who went into victims' homes and take care of them.

In 1688, after a fire that ravaged Québec City, citizens created the Bureau des Pauvres, an office composed of volunteers, who provided money, food and clothing to the victims.

The earliest volunteers served without pay in militia forces. The original term was coined in 1755, from the French word "voluntaire," defined as "one who offers himself for military service."

Benjamin Franklin founded the first volunteer firehouse in 1736. He took 30 men and formed the Union Fire Company in Philadelphia, PA. Many small towns and cities still have volunteer fire departments. More than 70% of all firefighters today are volunteers.

During the Revolutionary War, the famous "minute men" were a volunteer militia. Volunteers raised funds for the war efforts, showing their philanthropic attitude and patriotism. In the 1830s, young people got involved with outreach work through various religious organizations. Churches operated relief programs, helping the homeless and those victimized by unforeseen circumstances.

Volunteers also played a role in the Civil War. Groups such as Ladies' Aid Societies were created to make bandages, shirts, towels, bedclothes, uniforms and tents. The American Red Cross began during the Civil War, when Clara Barton took care of wounded soldiers. She recognized the need for medical nursing, supplies at the battlefronts and the need for morale boosts. The international Red Cross organization started in 1863 and encouraged Ms. Barton to create the American chapter. In 1881, she obtained formal recognition and served as its president until 1904. The organization's activities extended to floods, famines, fires and other disasters.

The YMCA was founded in 1844 in London, England, by George Williams, to provide healthy activities for men in cities. By 1851, the Young Men's Christian Association had spread throughout Europe and to the United States. Continued growth saw sports activities, fitness programs and activities geared at the entire family. In 1977, the YMCA was immortalized in a popular record by The Village People, with its accompanying dance becoming a craze that is still shared.

The YWCA was founded in 1855 in London, England, by Mary Jane Kennaird and Emma Roberts. YWCA USA was founded in 1858 and now has 300 associations serving 2.6 million people. Programs include health, fitness, aquatics, career nourishment, early childhood education, housing and shelter, economic empowerment and leadership development.

The Boys' Club was founded in 1860 in Hartford, Connecticut. In 1906, dozens of independent organizations joined as Federated Boys' Clubs. In 1990, they became Boys and Girls Clubs of America, providing after-school programs via 4,000 member clubs. This is the official charity of Major League Baseball.

A former club member, actor Denzel Washington, has been the organization's spokesperson since 1993.

The Salvation Army was founded in 1865 by William Booth in England to respond to conditions stemming from the industrial society. In 1880, the U.S. branch was formed by George Railton. The Army has worked to serve those most in need, combatting forces of evil.

Volunteers of America was founded in 1896 by Ballington and Maud Booth. They pledged to "go wherever we are needed, and do whatever comes to hand." In the early-1900s, they moved into tenement districts to care for people in poverty. They organized day nurseries and summer camps, provided housing for single men and women, and established halfway houses for released prisoners. During the Depression of the 1930s, VOA assisted people who were unemployed, hungry and homeless, establishing employment bureaus, wood yards, soup kitchens and food pantries where every food item cost one cent.

During wartime, VOA operated canteens, overnight lodging and meals for soldiers on leave. Affordable housing and child care were provided for defense industry workers. VOA headed community salvage drives during, collecting scrap metal, rubber and fiber for the war effort. VOA has since developed hundreds of affordable housing complexes. VOA operates nursing facilities, assisted and independent living residences.

Most volunteers of the 18th and 19th centuries found their assignments through churches and other private sector entities. People became sensitive to the plights of the disadvantaged. The late 1800s saw the rise of institutions becoming known for voluntary action. All were created to serve the needs of people in crisis of one kind or another. Some actually specialized in addressing specific causes.

Florence Nightingale was a nurse who helped improve hospital practices which improved patient survival rates. She worked in voluntary action from the Crimean War through World War I. Florence Nightingale's force of skilled nurses brought attention to needs of soldiers and affected healthcare in general.

The Salvation Army focused on unmarried people and alcoholism. The YMCA concentrated on improving men's economic opportunities. The Society of Saint Vincent de Paul developed voluntary services for the poor and homebound elderly.

In the 20th century, mainstream volunteer organizations began to flourish, shaping volunteer and non-profit organizations with the sole purpose of helping other organizations find their way. America was full of volunteers functioning in every region, giving others the chance at better lives.

Big Brothers and Big Sisters started in 1902 when Ernest Coulter, a clerk in New York Children's Court, befriended kids in need of positive influences. It was chartered in 1904, with each of 39 volunteers agreeing to befriend one child each. In 1934, President and Mrs. Franklin D. Roosevelt became patrons of the Big Brothers and Big Sisters Foundation. In 1958, the Big Brothers Association was charted by Congress. In 1970, Big Sisters International was incorporated. In 1977, both organizations merged.

The Boy Scouts were founded in 1907 in England by Robert Baden Powell. The American scouting program was founded in 1910. Its purpose was to "teach patriotism, courage, self-reliance and kindred values." Learning for Life is a school and work-site subsidiary program of BSA.

The NAACP was founded in Baltimore, MD, in 1909 by by Moorfield Storey, Mary White Ovington and W.E.B. Du Bois. The NAACP has addressed segregation, disfranchisement, social barriers, desegregation, civil rights, equal employment opportunities and educational initiatives, building coalitions worldwide.

The Girl Scouts were founded in 1912 by Juliette Gordon Low. That first chapter in Savannah, Georgia, has grown to 3.6 million members throughout the U.S. In 1917, a troop in Oklahoma began selling cookies at their local high school. In 1922, Girl Scouts of the USA recommended cookie sales, and a chapter in Philadelphia organized the first drive. Since then, each council has operated its own sales of cookies each year to raise funds in support of programs.

Camp Fire Girls was formed in 1912, as girls in Thetford, Vermont, watched males participate in outdoor activities through the Boy Scouts. The organization tried to merge with the Girl Scouts but continued as an independent entity. During World War I, Camp Fire Girls sold Liberty Bonds. They planted millions of trees and supported orphans. The name was changed to Camp Fire Boys and Girls in 1975, then in 2012 to Camp Fire.

The United Way was founded as Community Chest in Cleveland, OH, in 1913. There were 1,000 Community Chest organizations in 1948, when they were combined to form the United Foundation. The name United Way was adopted in 1963, modified to United Way of America in 1970. It is an umbrella organization, providing funding and support to thousands of non-profit organizations nationally.

Volunteer organizations drawing from business and citizenry include Rotary International, the Association of Junior Leagues, Kiwanis International, Lions International and the Exchange Clubs.

The first Volunteer Bureau was founded in Minneapolis, MN, in 1919 and became part of the Volunteer Center National Network, reaching 170 million people in thousands of cities across the nation.

Disabled American Veterans was founded by Robert Marx in Cincinnati, OH, in 1921. Marx had been injured during his World War I service. A women's auxiliary was formed in 1922. DAV was given a federal charter in 1932. DAV provides benefits assistance, outreach, research and advocacy.

Environmentalism also found its place during the 1930s, as President Franklin D. Roosevelt raised awareness by creating the Civilian Conservation Corps. The CCC planted 3 million trees in a single decade. Many green initiatives flourished over ensuing decades, a monumental event being Earth Day in 1970.

During World War II, volunteers were active in the military and on the home front. Volunteer organizations collected supplies, cared for the injured, entertained servicemen and supported civilians in a variety of ways.

After World War II, people shifted the focus of their altruistic passions to other areas, including helping the poor and volunteering overseas. The Peace Corps was founded in 1960. President Lyndon B. Johnson declared a War on Poverty in 1964, and volunteer opportunities expanded.

AmeriCorps is a national and community service organization. It has programs that address community needs in the areas of education, environment, public health and safety and disaster preparedness and response. It operates the Volunteers in Service to America (VISTA) program, initiated by LBJ's Economic Opportunity Act of 1964, the domestic version of the Peace Corps. Said Johnson: "Your Pay will be low. The conditions of your labor will be difficult. But you will have the satisfaction of leading a great national effort. And you will have the ultimate reward, which comes to those who serve their fellow man."

VISTA strives to "fight poverty with passion." Programs address illiteracy, health services, housing opportunities, community collaboration and efforts to break the poverty cycle. VISTA members complete the program with lessons learned in teamwork, leadership, responsibility and other life skills, carried with them for the rest of their lives.

National Volunteer Week began in 1974 as a way to recognize and celebrate the efforts of volunteers. Since then, the emphasis has widened to a nationwide effort to urge people to participate and volunteer in their communities. Every April, charities and communities reinforce the week's official theme ("Celebrating People in Action") by recognizing volunteers and fostering a culture of service. National Volunteer Week is sponsored by the Points of Light Institute, which began as a foundation, created in response to President George H.W. Bush's inaugural speech in 1989, urging volunteers and community activists to become "a thousand points of light."

Habitat For Humanity was founded in Americus, GA, in 1976. It has assisted more than four million people in the construction, rehabilitation and preservation of more than 800,000 homes. It is the largest non-profit building organization. Programs include A Brush with Kindness, mortgage assistance, Global Village Trips, RV Care-A-Vanners, Women Build, youth programs, recovery efforts along the Gulf Coast and Haiti, Collegiate Challenge and AmeriCorps Build-a-Thon.

In 1987, New York City launched CityCares, a program to get young professionals involved in volunteer service. The name was changed to the Hands on Network in 2004. It includes more than 70,000 corporate, faith and non-profit organizations, delivering 30 million hours of volunteer service each year.

Volunteer Match, a non-profit organization, was launched in 1998, a merger of Impact Online Inc. and Volunteer America. It utilized the newly emerging internet as an opportunity to match citizens interested in volunteering with organizations in their localities. It bundles enterprise tools with local, regional and national non-profit organizations, facilitating easy connections for those interested in serving. It has won awards as a useful resource and inspired greater usage of the internet by the non-profit sector. Worldwide Helpers is a comparable organization in the U.K.

VolunteerConnections.org was launched in 2000, later becoming 1-800-Volunteer.org. It features an online search for volunteer opportunities for individuals.

The Disabled Veterans National Foundation was created in 2007 by six women veterans and ever since has been helping men and women who have been wounded while on duty or have become sick during or after their service change their lives for the better. The DVNF provides services to disabled veterans and their families, collaborating with various organizations that can provide direct support. They have specific interest in helping those who suffer from Post Traumatic Stress Disorder as well as other brain injuries.

The Corporation for National and Community Service calculated in 2012 that 64.5 million Americans gave 7.9 billion hours of volunteer service.

Chapter 3

VOLUNTEERS, THE ART OF VOLUNTEERING

All good citizens want to get involved with worthwhile causes. Volunteers are the lifeblood of non-profit organizations and the causes they exemplify. The art of volunteering is in aligning with the community and investing one's time for maximum impact.

Volunteering has the power to improve the quality of life and health of those who donate their time. People must be performing the good deeds from a selfless nature. Volunteering improves not only the communities in which one serves, but also the life of the individual who is providing help to the communities.

Volunteering involves these types of investments:

- Time.
- Knowledge, skills, expertise.
- In-kind reciprocities.
- Political capital.
- Stakeholder relations.
- Social resources.

- Intellectual capital and heritage.
- Financial, directly or indirectly.

People volunteer because they believe in their communities and in specific causes. They want to give back, as time permits. They want to make a difference. Many volunteers get to utilize skills that their jobs do not allow, thus rounding them out professionally. There is a personal fulfillment that comes in unexpected ways. Plus, volunteering constitutes socialization, while doing good work on behalf of important causes.

During the course of each year, 26% of Americans regularly volunteer in their communities. So said the Current Population Survey of approximately 60,000 households that obtains information on the nation's civilian non-institutional population. Volunteers are defined as people who perform unpaid work (except for expenses) through or for an organization.

Volunteering is a core value of citizenship. By giving back, volunteers gain new skills, expand professional networks, stay connected to their community and enjoy physical and mental health benefits.

Categories of Volunteers

Community volunteering embodies those who work to improve their local quality of life. This activity occurs through non-profit organizations, local governments, churches, recreational groups, sports groups and community associations.

Service learning comes from travel to other lands. It involves students, Peace Corps workers and missionaries the opportunity to serve others, learn applicable lessons to bring home and serve as international goodwill ambassadors. Volunteers who travel to assist may learn foreign culture and language.

Virtual volunteering and micro volunteering are done through commitments from afar and involves small increments of time. They utilize the internet to involve volunteers from outside of the organization's geographical service area.

Environmental volunteering contributes toward environmental management or conservation. Volunteers conduct a range of activities including environmental monitoring, ecological restoration such as re-vegetation and weed removal, protecting endangered animals and educating others about the environment

Disaster relief volunteers play roles in the recovery effort following natural disasters, such as tsunamis, floods, droughts, hurricanes, and earthquakes. Volunteers form a laterally organized rapid-response team during and after the storms, from food to shelter to reconstruction. It is an example of mutualism at work, pooling resources and assistance.

School volunteering allows parents, students, neighbors and corporate supporters to support schools, giving assistance and resources beyond school budgets and classroom curriculum. In addition to the intangible rewards, volunteers can add the experiences to their resumes. Volunteering with schools can be an additional teaching guide for the students and help to fill the gap of local teachers.

Corporate volunteering is a wonderful way for companies to give back to the communities in which they do business. Many companies allow their employees to volunteer during work hours. These formalized Employee Volunteering Programs (EVPs), also called Employer Supported Volunteering (ESV), are regarded as a part of the companies' sustainability efforts, social responsibility and company marketing. EVPs building brand awareness and affinity, strengthen trust and loyalty among consumers, enhance corporate image and reputation, improve employee retention, increase employee productivity and loyalty and help companies to reach strategic goals. Research shows that employees who volunteer in the community are up to three times more effective and valuable to the companies.

Skills-based volunteer service involve organizers, who bring systems, checklists and accountabilities to tasks required. They include creative people who bring the vision, form and marketability to the causes and busy executives, who always find time for organizations committed to. Some skills-based volunteers are high-profile, whose names will attract other supporters for the organization, cause or event and those who receive name recognition for substantial donations.

Knowing more about your volunteers, what type they are and who works well together will enables organizations to utilize them more effectively, both for their good as well as the benefit of the organization.

Types of volunteer programs:

- Project.
- Internships.
- Conservation and environmental.
- Social.
- Fundraising.
- Recruitment and placement.
- Relief and emergency.
- Cause advocacy.
- Arts appreciation and advocacy.
- Healthcare focused.
- On-line volunteering.
- Micro-volunteering.
- The human condition.
- Skills transfer.
- Humanitarian.

Volunteer Recruitment and Retention

Questions that volunteers should ask themselves about the organization itself include:

- What are the organization's mission and goals?
- What is the organization's effectiveness in fulfilling its mission and attaining its goals?
- What kind of board do they have, how active are they and what is their tenure?
- Are there barriers to access of services from the organization?
- How well is the organization perceived?
- Is this a good organization with which you may be associated?
- What is the involvement of the community in the cause?

Questions that volunteers should ask themselves about volunteering:

- What selection criteria does the organization have when choosing volunteers?
- What kinds of people do they want as volunteers and over what period of time?
- Why has the project been set up?
- What are the conditions in which volunteers work?
- Can the organization put you in touch with previous volunteers?
- Can the organization give you details for your chosen assignment?
- Does the organization provide training and support for volunteers?
- Are there costs associated with the volunteer involvement?
- What is the organization's commitment to the needs and interests of volunteers?

Don't expect an announcement or a form letter to get large numbers of volunteers. Organizations must recruit key volunteers, with specific duties in mind. Each must cherry-pick the qualified volunteers in order to get maximum participation and longer-term involvement with the organization.

Strategies of attracting volunteers include:

- Warm-body recruitment.
- Targeted recruitment.
- Concentric circles recruitment.
- Attractor events.
- The scouting process.
- The nurturing process.

Recruitment strategies should capture attention, develop interest, gain approval for the cause and move volunteers to action. Tactics are the specific programs and activities that accomplish the recruitment and retention strategies. The range of possible tactics could include a recruitment brochure, personalized letters, advertisements, exhibits, reduced dues, introductory copies of a newsletter or annual report and a recruitment campaign. The best tactic is to utilize peer-to-peer communications.

Recruitment materials should reflect an identifiable image. Put a timetable to the organization's community outreach. Conduct sampling comparisons, varying only one component such as the timing.

No matter how typical or unusual are the tactics, each recruitment item should communicate one or more benefits of volunteering:

- Prestige.
- Recognition.
- Information on the benefiting cause.
- Networking opportunities.
- Opportunities to serve, including committee participation.
- Leadership by the organization, appreciating leadership qualities of volunteers.

Find creative partnerships in order to attract and keep volunteers. Other organizations will bring enthusiastic people with special skills. No organization can go it alone. Those who collaborate most often will be more successful with programs, volunteers and stakeholder outcomes. Loaves and Fishes is an agency in Sacramento, CA, that feeds the homeless. They run the Mustard Seed School for children of homeless families. This organization utilizes volunteers to manage the meals and school. They partner with local organizations, mostly churches.

Recruiting teams rather than individuals is particularly effective with younger volunteers. People are afraid of getting tied into a job for a lifetime and never being able to get out of it. When they volunteer together, they will stay committed longer, with such examples as Lawyers and Accountants for the Arts, Rotary House, corporate literacy coalitions, Lions Eye Bank and Thousand Points of Light teams.

When engaged, watch the trends and activities of those whom you have recruited. Volunteers are more willing to say yes to a short-term commitment with an end-date in sight. Volunteers have the opportunity to catch the vision of the organization because they were working with a good cause and passionate leadership. The leaders became mentors for future passion driven teams. Organizations are always looking for new leadership.

Supervising and maximizing the involvement of volunteers is vital. Clearly define job titles and responsibilities when recruiting volunteers. Be sure that they will be professionally supervised and that expectations are mutually agreed upon and communicated. The reason why people do not perform is that they do not know what is expected. Integrate volunteers into the flow of the organization, rather than compartmentalizing them against paid staff.

Find creative ways of thanking, acknowledging and commending volunteers more often. Find ways of inspiring teams and encouraging them to stay together.

Determine how and by whom the effectiveness of the recruitment and retention program will be measured. Determine the intervals at which results can be evaluated and to whom accountability will be reported. Ascertain how the program will be modified in order to make the best use of program results. The methods for evaluating the results need to be decided before the volunteer program is put into place, and the review becomes more systematic.

Most volunteer programs tend to focus more on recruitment, rather than retention. The tenets of a comprehensive recruitment campaign are more applicable to a retention program. Retention focuses more on follow-up, communication and interaction with volunteers who already are aware of what the organization has to offer. Recruitment and retention should be equally important. Ostensibly, it should be easier to keep volunteers than to recruit them.

Quotes About Volunteerism

"Everyone can be great because anyone can serve. You don't have to have a college degree to serve. You don't even have to make your subject and your verb agree to serve. You only need a heart full of grace and a soul generated by love."

—Dr. Martin Luther King, Jr.

"You cannot help someone get up a hill without getting closer to the top yourself."

—General H. Norman Schwarzkopf

"How wonderful it is that nobody need wait a single moment before starting to improve the world."
—**Anne Frank**, *Diary of a Young Girl*

"No man can become rich without himself enriching others."
—**Andrew Carnegie**

"The moral test of a society is how that society treats those who are in the dawn of life- the children; those who are in the twilight of life-the elderly; and those who are in the shadow of life-the sick, the needy and the handicapped."
—**Hubert Humphrey**

"We can do no great things, only small things with great love. There is a tremendous strength that is growing in the world through sharing together, praying together, suffering together and working together."
—**Mother Theresa**

"Never doubt that a small group of thoughtful, committed citizens can change the world; indeed, it's the only thing that ever has."
—**Margaret Mead**, anthropologist

"Volunteers are the only human beings on the face of the earth who reflect this nation's compassion, unselfish caring, patience, and just plain love for one another."
—**Erma Bombeck**

"The miracle is that the more we share, the more we have."
—**Leonard Nimoy**

"It is one of the most beautiful compensations of this life that no man can sincerely try to help another without helping himself. You cannot do a kindness too soon, for you never know how soon it will be too late."
—**Ralph Waldo Emerson**

"Never before has man had such a great capacity to control his own environment, to end hunger, poverty and disease, to banish illiteracy and human misery. We have the power to make the best generation of mankind in the history of the world."

—President John F. Kennedy

"He has a right to criticize, who has a heart to help. To ease another's heartache is to forget one's own."

—President Abraham Lincoln

"The best way to not feel hopeless is to get up and do something. Don't wait for good things to happen to you. If you go out and make some good things happen, you will fill the world with hope, you will fill yourself with hope."

—President Barack Obama

"Keep on sowing your seed, for you never know which will grow. Perhaps it all will."

—Ecclesiastes

"A hundred times every day, I remind myself that my inner and outer life depends on the labors of other men, living and dead, and that I must exert myself in order to give in the measure as I have received and am still receiving. Only a life lived for others is worth living."

—Albert Einstein

"Doing nothing for others is the undoing of ourselves."

—Benjamin Franklin

"I shall pass through this world but once. Any good therefore that I can do or any kindness that I can show to any human being, let me do it now. Let me not defer or neglect it, for I shall not pass this way again. The best way to find yourself, is to lose yourself in the service of others."

—Mahatma Gandhi

"If every American donated five hours a week, it would equal the labor of twenty million full-time volunteers. When you are kind to someone in trouble, you hope they'll remember and be kind to someone else. And it'll become like a wildfire."

—Whoopi Goldberg

"If you ever need a helping hand, it is at the end of your arm. As you get older you must remember you have a second hand. The first one is to help yourself. The second hand is to help others."

—Audrey Hepburn

"Whenever you are to do a thing, though it can never be known but to yourself, ask yourself how you would act were all the world looking at you and act accordingly. Every human being feels pleasure in doing good to another. May I never get too busy in my own affairs that I fail to respond to the needs of others with kindness and compassion."

—President Thomas Jefferson

"We cannot close ourselves off to information and ignore the fact that millions of people are out there suffering. I honestly want to help. I don't believe I feel differently from other people. I think we all want justice and equality, a chance for a life with meaning. All of us would like to believe that if we were in a bad situation someone would help us." ~Angelina Jolie

"The unselfish effort to bring cheer to others will be the beginning of a happier life for ourselves."

—Helen Keller

"It is from the numberless diverse acts of courage and belief that human history is shaped. Each time a man stands up for an ideal or acts to improve the lot of others or strikes out against injustice, he sends forth a tiny ripple of hope, and crossing each other from a million different centers of energy and daring, those ripples build a current that can sweep down the mightiest walls of oppression and resistance."

—Robert F. Kennedy

Chapter 4

CATEGORIES OF
NON-PROFIT ORGANIZATIONS

Non-profit organizations face many challenges beyond the scope of just providing core services. In the process of growth, membership, fund-raising, community relations, administrative and accountability activities, it is vital for each organization to ascertain its niche, constituent base, purpose and long-term potentiality.

I put together this analysis of non-profit organizations, having advised and worked with several hundred of them, at all sizes and stages of growth. This examination of the varying levels of non-profit organizations is for the purpose of pinpointing those unique probabilities, challenges and opportunities for the successful conduct of business.

1. Limited scope
Characteristics:
- Prompted by an impetus to form. Seemed like a good idea at the time.
- Often cater to the egos of founders.
- Not adept at fund-raising, marketing, board recruitment or volunteer retention.

- Fail to build support outside own nucleus.
- Entirely inner-focused.
- Limited impact and probably not long-lasting.

Fund Raising:
- Often exist hand-to-mouth.
- Individual-based.
- Little or no corporate support.
- Doesn't quite look good enough on paper to get second glances from funders.

Public Awareness:
- Very little.
- Leaders don't really understand the value and, thus, don't prioritize.
- No cohesive image. They view one article or one mention as a savior.

Board:
- Sparse, not a full working board.
- Gets whomever is available or most committed.
- No rules and responsibilities.
- Little accountability by board members, thus little productivity.
- High turnover.

Management:
- Volunteer.
- Inexperienced at non-profit organization administration.
- Cannot afford full-time staff.
- Non-centralized, often at odds with board members.

External Support:
- Little, outside board and contributors.
- Have not or will not build pockets of political and community support.
- Have not collaborated with other organizations toward common goals.

Non-Profit Standing:
- Not accorded foundation or corporate certification status.
- Never considered for important grants.
- Organization will always be in a tailspin, from crisis to crisis.

Examples:

- Small cottage foundations.
- Support mechanisms for persons afflicted with certain diseases.

2. Niche-cause

Characteristics:

- Organization has gone past the startup category (#1) and aspires to grow.
- Most remain true to mission and not seeking uncontrollable growth.
- Defined constituencies…don't presume to serve everybody.

Fund Raising:

- Have a few angels.
- Still not on the radar for foundations and corporate givers.
- May look good on paper, but need track record in order to attract major funding.

Public Awareness:

- Caught in a mindset that one article will magically do it all for the organization.
- Unsophisticated about value, usage and methodologies of public awareness.
- Differing viewpoints on this issue cause dissension among leaders.

Board:

- Junior executives on the boards, often their first board roles-responsibilities.
- No board development provided.
- Board routinely turns over, with little consistency.
- Those who control board often push own agendas.

Management:

- Part-time or single-staff. Might share executive director with other groups.
- Volunteers still handle most of the work.
- Scenario 1: executive director not the leader, takes assignments from the board.
- Scenario 2: executive director runs the show, keeping board members at bay.

External Support:

- Organization is inner-focused and does not reach to outside constituencies.
- Collaborate only when circumstances force the practice.

Non-Profit Standing:

- Not yet on the active radars of foundations or corporations.
- About half grow to the next level. The others wither or merge with other groups.

Examples:

- Child care councils, literacy provider agencies.

3. Advocacy

Characteristics:

- Growth is beyond geographical boundaries.
- Have multiple services, targeting defined, similar or related constituencies.
- Continue to develop additional services.

Fund Raising:

- Beginning to get attention for foundation grants, mostly the smaller ones.
- Beginning to attract corporate support, mostly in-kind services and volunteerism.
- Starting to amass good case studies, cases for support and grant proposal skills.

Public Awareness:

- Sometimes in the news but don't fully capitalize upon image opportunities.
- Think they cannot afford to market.

Board:

- These recruit members to serve, knowing they're the keys to successful growth.
- Mid-managers from business and advocate volunteers comprise the boards.
- Advocates and corporate volunteers often at odds about control of organization.

Management:
- Professional, full-time.
- Multiple professionals, with balanced staff.

External Support:
- Regular foundation bases of support.
- Often considered as viable organization for future foundation support.
- Beginning to receive public sector funding too.

Non-Profit Standing:
- Learn the difference between a hobbyist stance and a professional organization.
- Take steps to refine itself and become a longtime entity.

Examples:
- Small disease-oriented organizations
- School support-reform groups
- Small theatre groups

4. Emerging

Characteristics:
- These are the ones to watch. Many will have staying power.
- Some know their niche, refine their focus and stay lean.
- Others target strategically how they will grow.

Fund Raising:
- Beginning to attract family, estate and trust contributors.
- Maintain a small cadre of loyal benefactors.

Public Awareness:
- Image, name recognition and publicity become the primary focus.
- Services and community presence must have a distinct "point of difference."
- Continued refinement of branding and public perceptions will facilitate the future.

Board:
- Highly committed volunteers, some elected and some appointed.
- Cliques and issue-oriented contingencies vie for board control.
- Term-limited spots, with design for regular board turnover to bring in fresh faces.

Management:

- Have a professional management team.

External Support:

- Strong, loyal and renewable.

Non-Profit Standing:

- Have received good reviews and favorable ratings.
- Begin collaborating with other non-profit organizations.
- May be seen as umbrella organizations to other supporting constituencies.

Examples:

- Mid-sized provider organizations
- Niche-focused and small universities
- Mid-sized trade associations
- Leadership organizations

5. Midstream

Characteristics:

- Have proved themselves to go the distance.
- They plan, evaluate and function in a business-like manner.
- Generally well respected and maintain high levels of community involvement.

Fund Raising:

- Lots of ongoing special events.
- Regular corporate contributors.
- Regularly attract family, estate and trust contributors.

Public Awareness:

- High profile, out of necessity…more often for events than for programs.

Board:

- All elected, with prestige attached to selections.
- Board members get training and development on how to be most effective.

Management:

- Stable professional management team.
- Members are active, working closely with staff.

External Support:

- Strong, loyal and renewable.
- Possess skill at finding new pockets of funding, corporate support and grants.

Non-Profit Standing:
- Regularly partner with other public sector and non-profit entities.

Examples:
- Mid-sized universities,
- Large trade associations
- Muscular Dystrophy Association, Cystic Fibrosis, Multiple Sclerosis, etc.
- Mid-sized theatre groups, school boards

6. Mainstream

Characteristics:
- These are the ones that other non-profits look to as role models.
- They continually must evolve to next levels, never resting on well-earned laurels.

Fund Raising:
- Leadership knows that development is the lifeblood of the organization.
- One or two major annual events, plus secondary campaigns.
- Many individual and family givers.
- Many grants as source of support for defined projects, institutes and initiatives.

Public Awareness:
- Maintain a high profile, out of necessity, most often for programs and services.

Board:
- Upper management from corporations enthusiastically volunteer to serve.
- Board development is required and encouraged.

Management:
- Stable professional management team.
- Members are active, working closely with staff.

External Support:
- Strong, loyal and renewable.

Non-Profit Standing:
- Regularly audited, scrutinized and accountable for all actions.
- High goodwill, consistency and reputability based.

Examples:
- Major universities.
- Major theatre groups.
- Public television and radio.
- American Heart Association, American Cancer Society, etc.

7. Premium

Characteristics:
- These are the ones that other non-profits look to as role models.
- They continually must evolve to next levels, never resting on well-earned laurels.

Fund Raising:
- Development is a key responsibility for most of the leadership.
- Corporate culture revolves around fund-raising campaigns and giving issues.
- Have regular pockets of support, annual drives and secondary-support events.

Public Awareness:
- High profile, by design and out of necessity.

Board:
- Top echelon of community and business leaders jockey for seats on boards.
- Every board member has a job description, applicable skills and accountability.
- Board development is a primary activity, and board members continually evolve.

Management:
- Have a stable professional management team.
- Members are active, working closely with staff.

External Support:
- Strong, loyal and renewable.

Non-Profit Standing:
- Regularly audited, scrutinized and accountable for all actions.
- Highly goodwill, consistency and reputability based.

Examples:
- United Way, American Red Cross, etc.
- Major arts groups (opera, ballet, symphony).
- Tradition-tier universities.

Logos of prominent non-profit organizations.

Logos of prominent non-profit organizations.

Chapter 5

NON-PROFIT ORGANIZATIONS

Key Terms, Trends, Challenges, Opportunities

Non-profit organizations are a phenomenon of the last 100 years. Prior to the IRS non-profit designation, organizations providing charitable, educational and community services came under the purview of business or government.

When the U.S. Congress enacted the income tax in 1913, it created the 501 code, which gave tax-exempt status to organizations with defined purposes and intents.

This gave rise to the establishment of non-profit organizations, whose numbers have steadily grown. Their missions and service reaches have grown exponentially.

Section 501(c) of the U.S. tax code has 29 sections, listing specific conditions that organizations must meet in order to be considered tax-exempt under the section. These are:

501(c)(1) — Corporations organized under acts of Congress, such as federal credit unions

501(c)(2) — Title holding corporations for exempt organizations

501(c)(3) — Charitable, non-profit, religious and educational organizations

501(c)(4) — Political education organizations

501(c)(5) — Labor unions and agriculture

501(c)(6) — Business league and chamber of commerce organizations

501(c)(7) — Recreational club organizations

501(c)(8) — Fraternal beneficiary societies

501(c)(9) — Voluntary employee beneficiary associations

501(c)(10) — Fraternal lodge societies

501(c)(11) — Teachers' retirement fund associations

501(c)(12) — Life insurance associations, mutual irrigation and telephone companies

501(c)(13) — Cemetery companies

501(c)(14) — Credit unions

501(c)(15) — Mutual insurance companies

501(c)(16) — Corporations organized to finance crop operations

501(c)(17) — Employee associations

501(c)(18) — Employee-funded pension trusts created before June 25, 1959

501(c)(19) — Veterans' organizations

501(c)(20) — Group legal services plan organizations

501(c)(21) — Black lung benefit trusts

501(c)(22) — Withdrawal liability payment fund

501(c)(23) — Veterans' organizations created before 1880

501(c)(24) — Trusts under the Employee Retirement Income Security Act

501(c)(25) — Title-holding corporations for other qualified exempt organizations

501(c)(26) — High-risk health coverage organizations

501(c)(27) — Workers' compensation reinsurance organizations

501(c)(28) — National railroad retirement trust

501(c)(29) — Qualified non-profit health insurance issuers

501(d) — Religious and apostolic associations

501(e) — Cooperative hospital service organizations

501(f) — Cooperative service organizations of educational institutions

501(g) — Agricultural (cultivating land, harvesting crops, raising livestock)

501(h) — Certain lobbying activities by a non-profit organization

501(i) — Certain social clubs

501(j) — Training athletes for events like the Olympics

501(k) — Child care organizations

501(l) — Government corporations exempt under subsection (c)(1)

501(m) — Organizations providing insurance not exempt from tax

501(n) — Charitable risk pools

501(o) — Hospitals participating in provider-sponsored organizations

501(p) — Suspension for terrorist activities

501(q) — Special rules for credit counseling organizations

Key Terms

Non-Profit and Not-for-Profit are comparable terms, describing organizations that do not redistribute surplus funds to owners or shareholders. The redistribute funds back into programs and services.

Non-governmental organizations (NGOs) are citizen associations that operate independently of governments. They deliver resources or serve social or political purposes. Examples include CARE, UNICEF and the World Bank. Operational NGOs are primarily concerned with development projects. Advocacy NGOs are primarily concerned with promoting causes. Variations of NGOs include:

- BINGO (business-friendly international NGO), such as the Red Cross.
- ENGO (environmental NGO), such as the World Wildlife Fund.

- GONGO (government-operated NGO), organizations created by government to further certain agendas.
- INGO (international NGO), such as Oxfam.
- QUANGO (quasi-autonomous NGO), such as the International Standards Organization (ISO). Its standards are voluntary, and many of its members are part of the governmental structures of their countries. ISO standards have found their way into many laws and business practices.
- RINGO (religious international NGO), such as the Catholic Relief Services.
- DONGO (Donor Organized NGO).
- TANGO (technical assistance NGO).
- MANGO (market advocacy NGO).

The Executive Director is often referred to as the CEO, the head of each non-profit organization.

The Development Director is the highest fund development staff position. Fund Development is the process of cultivating relationships with people who will support a non-profit organization. Cultivation is defined as an activity that builds awareness and connection for donors and funders with the organization, and increases its understanding of why someone might give to the organization. Fund Development includes the specific methods used to secure charitable donations, including annual fund, face-to-face asks, online, proposals, etc..

The Culture of Philanthropy is familiar to fund-raising professionals. The Culture of Philanthropy refers to a set of organizational values and practices that support and nurture development within a non-profit organization. Everyone promotes philanthropy and can articulate a case for giving. Fund Development is valued as a mission-aligned program of the organization. Organizational systems are established to support donors. The executive director is committed and personally involved in fund-raising.

Non-profit Enterprise involves organizations generating earned income, as opposed to donated income. Strategies could include business ventures, program related products, program related services, hard property, soft property cause-related marketing and licensing.

Stakeholders are persons and organizations that affect you, might help or hurt your cause and who would benefit from knowing about your work.

Trends, Challenges, Opportunities

People who work for non-profit organizations are a special and dedicated breed. Many have diverse business careers but have a "calling" when it comes to non-profit service. Most agencies do remarkable things on razor-thin budgets. Each employee is accountable and makes a difference in the whole organization. Non-profit staffs generally have great rapport with volunteers, collectively making an impact in the organizations' missions.

Non-profit organizations face great challenges, including:

- Mission focus.
- Fundraising is fundamental.
- A better board makes you better.
- Nothing succeeds like success.
- Fiscal stress.
- Increased demand for services as the population increases, plus the changing demographics of those served.
- Increased competition. The number of non-profit organizations has increased 60% in the last decade, fueled by social media.
- Increased pressure to perform.
- Human resources stretched and often burned out.
- The need for greater visibility and spreading the word.
- The need to establish creative partnerships.
- Establishing a development culture.
- Finding the necessary funds.
- Finding committed and active volunteers.
- Doing more with limited resources.
- Competition from a proliferated field of agencies.

- Duplication of services by many agencies.
- Need to merge and combine efforts.
- Need to collaborate better.
- Thousands more starting each year.
- Competition for funds, community support, volunteers and recognition.
- Ripple effect of years without resources.
- Increased needs in communities, due to the recession, population bursts.

There exist 1.4 million non-profit organizations in the United States, generating more than one trillion dollars. Non-profits comprise 8% of the workforce across the nation. Because of how quickly it has grown, the sector is now suffering from a lack of standards and codes of conduct. The sector is not unified and often weak in public policy. Leadership most needed.

Trends and opportunities facing non-profit organizations:

- Greater government funding to non-profit organizations.
- Growth across borders, expanded service areas.
- Participation in regional and national networks.
- Selling of services to corporate constituencies.
- Sustainability.
- Competition for the best development directors.
- High turnover in development directors.
- Unrealistic performance standards.
- Organizations running more on ego and reaction than firm strategy.
- Board involvement in fund raising is low.
- Finding the best board members is a challenge.
- Different generations have different commitments to non-profit organizations and community involvement.
- Limited experience with partnerships.
- Many organizations have a culture that does not support fundraising success.

Here are some recommendations:

- Embrace social media.
- Overcome a fear of change.
- Strengthen and diversify the talent pool.
- Maximize the use of your resources.
- Embrace fund development.
- Elevate the field of fund-raising.
- Conduct better board development.
- Invest in grantee fund-raising capacity.
- Conduct online fund-raising.
- Leverage technological innovation.
- Embrace creativity.
- Set realistic goals.
- Share accountability.

Public Service Leadership

Government service represents a calling. Elected officials run for office and maintain staffs who interface regularly with communities. Citizens are appointed to commissions and boards at the federal, state and local levels, drawing upon their expertise to serve governmental entities.

Educators serve the community at all levels. Teachers constitute the frontline influence on youth. School district administrators hold the public trust to deliver services, shepherd the resources and remain accountable. Citizens run for school boards as parents and community leaders.

Associations represent a variety of professions, causes, geographic areas, historical sectors, homeowner zones and community niches. Leaders in those associations organize to achieve objectives and get actions. They are combinations of volunteers, professional resources and stakeholders from throughout communities.

Chambers of commerce are regional in nature and advocate for business opportunities. They take on marketing roles for their region and enjoy the volunteer cooperation of leading community figures. They host meetings, community structures and special events such as "business after hours."

Economic development entities embrace research, planning, strategy and advocacy on behalf of regional areas, most notably municipalities. They work in cooperation with chambers of commerce, elected officials, community groups and associations to achieve mutually beneficial goals.

Professional alliances bring businesses and their associations into cooperation on targeted projects. They often come together for specific time frames and go their separate ways when the work is done. Most participants find themselves in other professional alliances as situations warrant. They find that collaborating achieves the kind of results that individual players cannot necessarily achieve on their own.

Umbrella groups support non-profit organizations and provide funding and volunteer corps. Examples are umbrella groups in the areas of literacy, drug abuse, hunger, education, disease prevention, special populations advocacy and support of the arts. United Way is a major umbrella group that provides resources to member agencies, as well as grants for special projects of other non-profit entities.

Many healthcare institutions are non-profit. They are engaged in patient care, hospitals, research and community service. Some are administered by foundations and faith-based organizations. All hold non-profit charters and function with transparency while interfacing with stakeholders. Some maintain for-profit units.

Volunteers serve public service programs, just as they do with 501(c)(3) non-profit organizations. They bring talents and perspectives that compliment the elected officials and program administrators.

Persons who participate in Public Service Leadership generally hold commitments to make a difference, stand for something and leave a legacy.

Increasing Employee Effectiveness

Employees don't perform well because of the following circumstances:

1. They don't know why they should do it.
2. They don't know where to begin and end.

3. They don't know what they are supposed to do.
4. They don't know how to do it.
5. They think they are doing it.
6. They think their way is better than what the boss or the rules suggest.
7. Something else is more important to them.
8. They are not rewarded for doing…just punished for not doing.
9. They are rewarded for not doing it…and punished for doing it.
10. They think they cannot do the tasks at hand or are not up to bigger challenges.

This is why we don't get profitable action from employees:

1. The organization does not plan for change or success.
2. People do not identify with objectives of the organization. Just work for a paycheck.
3. People are not empowered to feel important as contributors toward desired results.
4. People are not sure where they fit into the overall structure and mission.
5. Follow-up systems are not implemented.
6. People do not clearly understand what they are expected to do.
7. Goals are either too large or non-communicated.
8. Managers do not set enough of an example.

This is how to get profitable action from employees:

1. Know the organization's mission, goals, tactics and methods to achieve results.
2. Know job responsibilities, performance standards and contributions toward total effort.
3. Communicate all the procedures, regulations, scope of work and ramifications.
4. Give consistent discipline and support for correct actions. Assure there is accountability for mistakes, plus fair and consistent supervision.

5. Be sure that training is provided and that latitude is given to exercise judgment, supported by management.
6. Allow employees to fit into the strategy, where everyone expresses ideas and suggestions, and people mentor others, learning from experiences.
7. Empower employees to do something worthwhile.

Customer Focused Management

In today's highly competitive environment, every dynamic of a successful organization must be geared toward ultimate customers. Customer focused management goes far beyond just smiling, answering queries and communicating with buyers. It transcends service and quality. Every organization has customers, clients, stakeholders, financiers, volunteers, supporters or other categories of "affected constituencies."

Organizations must change their focus from products and processes to the values which they share with customers. Everyone with whom you conduct business is a customer or referral source of someone else. The service that we get from some people, we pass along to others. Customer service is a continuum of human behaviors, shared with those whom we meet.

Customers are the lifeblood of every business. Employees depend upon customers for their paychecks. Yet, you wouldn't know the correlation when poor customer service is rendered. Employees of many companies behave as though customers are a bother, do not heed their concerns and do not take suggestions for improvement.

There is no organization that cannot undergo some improvement in its customer orientation. Being the recipient of bad service elsewhere must inspire us to do better for our own customers. The more that one sees poor customer service and customer neglect in other companies, we must avoid the pitfalls and traps in our own companies.

Do you ever try to complain about poor customer service, and the total lack of empathy made you further angry than when you contacted them in the first place? Companies tend to rationalize that lost customers are easily replaceable. Research shows that retaining 2% of your customers from leaving or deflecting their business has a bigger effect upon your bottom line than cutting operating costs by 10%.

A longtime steady customer is three times more profitable for the business than a recently added customer. Longtime customers make referrals, which reduce the company's marketing costs. Dissatisfied customers will tell 10-20 other people.

Employees mirror management's philosophy. If they are only concerned with the cash register ringing, without giving any more, than they do not have a right to keep customers or stay in business. Those who think and behave as though customers are necessary evils and tolerate them accordingly, exemplify a mindset that decimates goodwill.

If problems are handled only through form letters, subordinates or call centers, then management is the real cause of the problem. Customer focused management begins and ends at top management. Management should speak personally with customers, to set a good example for employees. If management is complacent or non-participatory, then it will be reflected by behavior and actions of the employees.

Organizations should coordinate relationship management skills into its overall corporate strategy, in order to satisfy customer needs profitably, draw together the components for practical strategies and implement strategic requirements to impact the business.

Any company can benefit from having an advisory board, which is an objective and insightful source of sensitivity toward customer needs, interests and concerns. The successful business must put the customer into a co-destiny relationship. Customers want to build relationships, and it is the obligation of the business to prove that it is worthy.

Customer focused management is the antithesis to the traits of bad business, such as the failure to deliver what was promised, bait and switch advertising and a failure to handle mistakes and complaints in a timely, equitable and customer-friendly manner.

Don't post a Customer Service Index (CSI) rating unless you and every member of your team really know what it means. There must be a commitment to maintain it. Consumer complaints must launch a genuine action to improve. To avoid customer concerns and do business as usual is a mockery of the quality process. Such a company does not have the right to flaunt its perceived CSI rating any longer.

Customer focused management is dedicated to providing members with an opportunity to identify, document and establish best practices through benchmarking to increase value, efficiencies and profitability.

Chapter 6

MEMORIES, EVENTS, NOSTALGIA

Contributions to Humanitarian and Community Service

A cademic competitions had their roots in school spelling bees. They united colleges around knowledge and teams of students. They were exemplified by the "General Electric College Bowl" on CBS-TV (hosted by Allen Ludden) and the "Texaco Star National Academic Championship."

Adopt-a-Pet programs are conducted by the Society for Prevention of Cruelty to animals. They have drives and often showcase pets on local TV shows as part of their community outreach. SPCA was founded in London, England, in 1824. It is a global animal welfare organization, operating programs on animal welfare, assisting in cruelty to animal cases and finding new homes for unwanted animals.

The American Association of Retired Persons (AARP) was founded by Dr. Ethel Percy Andrus in Ojai, CA, in 1958. Its programs include advocacy, lobbying and services to persons over the age of 50. Its motto is "to serve, not to be served."

The American Foundation for the Blind was organized in Vinton, IA, in 1921. It has advocated legislation and access to help persons with vision loss. It is the largest producer of braille writers and talking books. Helen Keller dedicated her life to working with AFB. The Foundation works with technology companies, making products more accessible by those with vision limitations.

The Anti-Defamation League was founded by the Independent Order of B'Nai B'rith in 1913. Its goals and programs strive to fight anti-semitism, bigotry, terrorism, persecution and discrimination. It defends civil rights and democratic ideals.

The Better Business Bureau was founded in 1912. Its goals are to advance marketplace trust, expose frauds, promote business efficiencies, encourage ethical conduct of business and celebrate excellent customer service. It has educational programs, rating system, dispute resolution, professional development and awards recognition through its chapters.

Black History Month was launched in 1926 as Negro History Week, coinciding with Black commemorations of the birthdays of Abraham Lincoln and Frederick Douglass. By the 1970s, it evolved into Black History Month.

Blood banks take donations from individuals, storing the blood for future transfusions, in order to save lives. John Braxton Hicks first experimented with chemical methods of preventing coagulation of blood in the 1890s. The first transfusion was performed by Dr. Albert Hustin and Dr. Luis Agote in 1914. The British Red Cross established the first blood donor service in 1921. One of the first blood banks was founded in Barcelona, Spain, in 1936. Dr. Bernard Fanfus began the first hospital blood bank in Chicago, IL, in 1937. The Blood for Britain campaign in 1940 took collections in the U.S. and provided them to the U.K. The plastic bag for blood collection was introduced in 1950. Collection and distribution programs now exist in every community around the world.

Boys and Girls Clubs of America was founded in Hartford, CT, in 1860. In 1906, 53 independent clubs joined to form a national organization. There are now 4,000 local clubs.

Boys State and Girls State are summer leadership camps, sponsored by the American Legion. Boys State was created in 1935, and Girls State was created in

1938. High school students are nominated, participating at state and national levels. Famous alumni of the leadership program include Garth Brooks, Jon Bon Jovi, Roger Ebert, Jane Pauley, Scott Bakula, Bill Clinton, Rush Limbaugh, Beau Biden, Nancy Redd and Tom Brokaw.

CARE was founded 1945 as the Cooperative for Assistance and Relief Everywhere. It is a non-partisan non-government agency. It began by sending CARE packages to countries in Europe who were torn by war. CARE expanded the globe, assisting areas in need with food, supplies and diplomatic service. CARE has helped construct schools and provided philanthropic services across the globe. Empty Plate Day was one of the first online fundraising initiatives, operated by CARE International.

The Children's Defense Fund is a child advocacy and research group, founded in 1973 by Marian Wright Edelman. It provides a voice for children who cannot vote, lobby or speak for themselves, fostering youth leadership programs.

The Cystic Fibrosis Foundation was organized in Philadelphia, PA, in 1955. It awards research grants for studying cystic fibrosis, a genetic disorder that affects the lungs, pancreas, liver, kidneys and intestine.

Earth Day was first held on April 22, 1970, and has been observed on the same day ever since. Events show support for environmental protection. It is now celebrated in 193 countries globally.

Easter Seals was founded in 1919 as the National Society for Crippled Children. The organization assists children and adults with physical and mental disabilities, plus special needs. Services include medical rehabilitation, residential, job training and employment, child care, adult day care, camping, recreation and substance abuse programs.

Food for Thought was a collaborative program combining hunger and illiteracy services. It was jointly sponsored by the Houston Food Bank and the Houston READ Commission.

In 1917, a Girl Scouts troop in Oklahoma began baking shortbread cookies in a mother's kitchen and sold the cookies at their local high school. In 1922, Girl Scouts of the USA recommended cookie sales, and a chapter in Philadelphia organized the first drive. Since then, each council has operated its own sales of cookies each year to raise funds in support of programs.

Hotlines were prolific in the 1960s and 1970s. This was pre-internet, and telephones were the medium for people in crisis to call and talk with volunteer counselors. Hotlines served teens, those with drug dependencies and families in crisis.

The Job Corps was created in 1964 under the Economic Opportunity Act. Sargent Shriver was the first director. It helps young people (ages 18-24) to receive vocational and academic training, thus improving the quality of life. The Job Corps is now administered under the Workforce Investment Act of 1998.

Junior Achievement was founded in 1919 by Horace Moses, Theodore Vail and Winthrop Crane, in Springfield, Massachusetts. It works with local business in delivering programs on entrepreneurship, financial literacy and work readiness. In 1975, JA introduced its in-school program, Project Business.

Just Say No to Drugs originated in a substance abuse prevention program by the National Institutes of Health. First Lady Nancy Reagan embraced the program since hearing about it on a campaign appearance in 1980. She was visiting a school in California in 1982 and was asked by a student what to do if she was offered drugs. Mrs. Reagan responded: "Just say no," and it became the slogan for the public awareness campaign. More than 5,000 Just Say No clubs were established in schools and youth organizations. Just Say No was utilized in the U.K. as well.

The League of Nations was created under the Treaty of Versailles in 1920. Its mission was to maintain world peace. It championed such issues as collective security, disarmament, labor conditions, global health, human and drug trafficking and minority rights protection. The United Nations replaced it in 1946.

The League of Women Voters was founded by Carrie Chapman Catt in 1920 during a meeting of the National American Woman Suffrage Association. It hosts forums, debates and policy institutes nationally to inform voters on the candidates and issues in election cycles.

Lemonade Day is an annual event to empower children into entrepreneurship and business. It was begun by Michael Holthouse in 2007 in Houston, TX, and has spread to serve one million kids across North America.

The Leukemia & Lymphoma Society was founded by Rudolph and Antoinette de Villiers in White Plains, NY, in 1949. It is a voluntary health organization dedicated to funding blood cancer research, education and patient services.

Little League Baseball was founded in 1939 in Williamsport, PA. It organizes sports programs nationally and hosts the Little League World Series each August in Williamsport.

The Make a Wish Foundation was founded in 1980 in Phoenix, Arizona. It arranges experiences for children aged 3-17 with life-threatening conditions, referred by physicians. Wishes are granted through 61 chapters. Professional wrestler John Cena holds the record for the most wishes granted (450), followed by Justin Bieber and the National Women's Collegiate Fraternity Chi Omega.

The marathon was one of the original Olympic Games events in 1896 and was standardized in 1921. More than 500 cities hold marathon races for runners, including Boston, New York, Washington, Houston, New York City, Detroit, Niagra Falls, Chicago, Tibet, The Great Wall of China, Berlin, London, Tokyo and Warsaw.

McGruff the Crime Dog was created for the Advertising Council and in public service announcements says "take a bite out of crime." He has appeared since 1978 for the National Crime Prevention Council.

The Multiple Sclerosis Society was founded in 1946. It supports research, professional education and treatment in the area of multiple sclerosis, a disease in which insulating covers of nerve cells in the brain and spinal cord are damaged.

The Olympic Games originated in 1896 in Athens, Greece. 241 athletes representing 14 nations competed in 43 events. The games were held in Paris in 1900 and St. Louis in 1904. The Winter Games were first staged in 1908 and became an ongoing event in 1924. The games have economic and social impact on host nations, as well as rallying morale and support throughout the world.

Here are some business take-backs that may be interpreted through the prism of the Olympic Games:

- Grabbing your own gold means different things to different people.
- We must celebrate the journey, the hard work and the process of getting there, not just the moment of glory.
- Having people believing in you makes all the difference.
- True champions will support and nurture others.
- No champion made it without good coaching. Having a qualified, experienced mentor is the sure path to your success.

The Peace Corps was originally suggested by Rep. John F. Kennedy in 1951. He said: "Young college graduates would find a full life in bringing technical advice and assistance to the underprivileged and backward Middle East. In that calling, these would follow the constructive work done by the religious missionaries in these countries over the past 100 years." Senator Hubert H. Humphrey, Jr. (D-Minnesota) introduced the first bill to create the Peace Corps in 1957. During the 1960 Presidential campaign, Kennedy endorsed the concept, calling it the Peace Corps. In his inaugural speech, Kennedy made the Peace Corps a reality, saying: "Ask not what your country can do for you. Ask what you can do for your country." Kennedy appointed Sargent Shriver as the first director. Peace Corps volunteers now work in 69 countries. AmeriCorps VISTA is a program to reduce poverty. It began in 1964 as a domestic version of the Peace Corps.

Police Week thanks officers for their service and commemorates police who have died in the line of duty. The Memorial takes place on May 15, during Police Week. The event is sponsored by the National Fraternal Order of Police and is implemented by the National FOP Memorial Committee. Events of National Police Week include the annual Blue Mass, Candlelight Vigil, Wreath Laying Ceremony, National Police Survivors Conference, Honor Guard Competition and the Emerald Society & Pipe Band March and Service. The order creating it was signed by President John F. Kennedy in 1962. The national events draw law enforcement officers and their families to Washington, D.C. each year.

Prejudice Awareness Summits are held in conjunction with Jewish Women International. Co-hosted by schools and congregations, the summits are day-long conferences studying racism, prejudice and opportunities for young people to learn community acceptance and collaboration skills.

The President's Council on Youth Fitness, Sports and Nutrition was founded in 1956 to encourage American children to be healthy and active by President Dwight D. Eisenhower. In 1963, President John F. Kennedy changed the name to President's Council on Physical Fitness, to serve all Americans. In 1966, President Lyndon B. Johnson created the President's Challenge Youth Physical Fitness Awards Program. In 1983, Congress declared May as National Physical Fitness and Sports Month. In 2010, President Barack Obama renamed the agency the President's Council on Fitness, Sports and Nutrition.

Private Sector Initiatives was created as a task force by President Ronald Reagan in 1981 to advise the President, the Secretary of Commerce, and other agencies on ways to develop and encourage private sector leadership and responsibility for meeting public needs. Many of its tenets were later adopted by Thousand Points of Light.

Sal and Arnie were characters who appeared in public service announcements for the U.S. Department of Agriculture. They discussed guidelines for the clean and healthy preparation of food.

Salk Vaccinations were public immunization shots against polio, offered in schools during the 1950s and 1960s. Jonas Salk (1914-1995) was a medical researcher and virologist. He discovered and developed the first effective polio vaccine. His books included "Man Unfolding," "Survival of the Wisest," "World Population and Human Values" and "Anatomy of Reality: Merging of Intuition and Reason." His last years were spent in researching a vaccine for HIV.

School reform programs stimulate the curriculum, so that kids complete high school and go on to college. James Ketelsen put his retirement wealth to good purpose. As Chairman and CEO of Tenneco, he supported many causes, including a scholarship program began in 1989 at Jeff Davis High School in Houston, TX. Working with Jeff Davis, Ketelsen learned that one needed to reach kids long before high school, in order to encourage them to stay in school and become good citizens. His foundation realized that every school in the feeder pattern needed to benefit from Project GRAD (Graduation Really Achieves Dreams). The result is a system of curricular, methodological, and student and family support programs that help build academic skills, improve student behavior, address family needs and set children on the road to college. The foundation provides training and support to classroom teachers, along with reading, math and classroom management (leadership) curricula.

Smokey the Bear has represented the United States Forest Service since 1944. He was created by the Advertising Council, portraying Smokey as an orphaned cub in the aftermath of forest fires. He proclaims: "Only you can prevent forest fires." Lyrics to his song: "Smokey the Bear. Prowling and growling and sniffing the air. He can find a fire before it starts to flame. That's why they call him Smokey. That was how he got his name. He will let you take his honey and pretend he's not so smart. But don't you harm his trees, for he's a ranger in his heart."

Special Olympics was founded in 1968 by Eunice Kennedy Shriver. Special Olympics is the largest sports activity for children and adults with disabilities. More than 94,000 events are held each year in 170 countries, with competitions attracting 4.5 million participants.

Sunshine Kids was founded by Rhonda Tomasco in Houston, TX, in 1982. It offers programs for children who are undergoing cancer treatment at hospitals across the U.S. It hosts hospital parties, community events, letter signings and other signs of encouragement to children.

Take Our Sons and Daughters to Work Day was created in 1992 by the Ms. Foundation for Women. It occurs each year on the fourth Thursday of April. 37 million children now visit workplaces in 200 countries.

Teen Canteens evolved in the 1950s, as churches and community associations strove to offer positive activities for youth, as the alternative to juvenile delinquency. From these sprung Teen Challenge, a variety of youth leadership programs.

Thousand Points of Light began as a speech line by George H.W. Bush at the 1988 Republican National Convention. As President of the U.S., Bush developed the concept of volunteering and community service, extending it to a non-profit foundation after his presidency. Points of Light now has 250 affiliates in 30 countries, plus partnerships with many non-profit organizations and companies.

The United Nations was founded on October 24, 1945, replacing the League of Nations. It promotes international cooperation among 193 member countries. It is headquartered in New York City, with offices in Geneva, Nairobi and Vienna. Its objectives are the maintenance of international peace and security, protecting human rights, spurring economic development, fostering social rights, shepherding the environment and distributing humanitarian aid. Its divisions are the General Assembly, Security Council, Economic and Social Council, Secretariat, International Court of Justice and the Trusteeship Council. UN System agencies include the World Bank Group, World Health Organization, World Food Program, UNESCO and UNICEF.

UNICEF was founded in 1946 as the United Nations Children's Fund, providing food and healthcare services to war-torn countries. The organization is known for its "Trick Or Treat" program, where children collect money for humanitarian service. Programs support children's rights, corporate responsibility and food distribution. The Campaign for Child Survival sought to save children's lives in underdeveloped nations, utilizing the concepts of growth monitoring, oral rehydration, breast-feeding of infants and immunizations. I worked with two of UNICEF's goodwill ambassadors: Vincent Price (on the Campaign for Child Survival) and Audrey Hepburn (on (hunger and literacy initiatives).

In communities across the world, local and national causes benefit from citizen participation at all levels. With the support of corporations, they support a host of charitable events, including:

Art festivals
Awards programs
Dog shows
Dress for success programs
Christmas drives
Cinco de Mayo
Community re-development
Environmental cleanups

Ethnic appreciation, cultural and awareness events

Family outreach initiatives

Fireworks shows

Food drives and pantries

Fun runs and walkathons

Golf Tournaments

Health screenings

Healthy baby initiatives

Hire veteran programs

Holiday feasts

Holiday lighting events

Home tours

Horse shows

House construction for low-income families

Immunizations and vaccinations

International festivals

Literacy fairs, festivals and reading events

Medical screenings

Museum days, tours and festivals

Neighborhood watch programs, such as Night Out from Crime

New citizen admittance programs

Nutrition campaigns

Organ donor campaigns

Parades

Patriotic events

Pet adoption campaigns

Prison programs

Read-a-Thons

Robotics competitions

Safety campaigns

School carnivals and festivals

School park programs

School savings programs

Science fairs

Senior citizen programs

Spay and neutering programs

Tennis tournaments

Theatre days, tours and festivals

United Way campaigns

Veterans Day parades, festivals and educational events

Vision screenings

Volunteer fairs

Voter campaigns

Youth programs: Camps, Leadership Programs, Sports Competitions

Music Themed Events

Bob Geldof is a rock star, leader of the group The Boomtown Rats. He was the driving force behind "Band Aid" in 1984. It was a record featuring the talents of most major British rock stars, to raise funds to assist famine relief in Ethiopia. The song was titled "Do They Know It's Christmas?" Geldof was one of the organizers of the Live Aid concert, a 16-hour extravaganza to raise money and awareness for Africa. He became involved in the work of non-governmental organizations and was the leading spokesperson on Third World debt and relief.

Inspired by the work of Geldof and Band Aid, a group of American recording artists organized by Michael Jackson, Kenny Rogers and Lionel Richie supported USA for Africa. A total of 47 top stars recorded the song "We Are the World." That hit record raised funds for relief of famine and disease in Africa.

"Hands Across America," a chain of national events and benefit concert followed. On May 25, 1986, 6.5 million people held hands for 15 minutes along a path from New York City to Long Beach, CA, across the U.S. The record and concert raised more than $100 million for the humanitarian programs of USA for Africa.

Farm Aid was organized by Willie Nelson, John Mellencamp and Neil Young. Farm Aid concerts have continued every year since 1985.

Live Aid was a benefit concert held July 13, 1985, at both Wembley Stadium in London (attended by 72,000) and John F. Kennedy Stadium in Philadelphia (attended by 100,000). It was organized by Bob Geldof and Midge Ure to raise funds for the Ethiopian famine.

"Music Freedom Day" takes place on March 3 each year. It celebrates freedom of expression, recognizing forces that might suppress musicians. The 2016 event honored the victims of terrorist attacks in Paris, France, in November 2015.

These charity concerts and campaigns were in the tradition of others: John Lennon's 1969 "Give Peace a Chance," George Harrison's 1972 "Concert for Bangladesh," the 1979 "No Nukes Concert" and "Voices That Care."

Entertainers have appeared regularly on telethons. One of the earliest was the "Jim Moran Cancer Fund Benefit," 1950 on WENR-TV, the ABC affiliate in Chicago, IL, featuring Don McNeill, Johnny Desmond, Sam Cowling and Patsy Lee.

One of the earliest national fundraising spectaculars was the "Easter Seals Teleparade of Stars," 1955. It starred Jack Benny, Shirley MacLaine, Van Johnson, Ruth Hussey, Liberace, Robert Sterling, Anne Jeffries, Bob Crosby, The Modernaires, Dick Contino, Kitty Kallen, Don Wilson, Paul Baron orchestra. It was a benefit for Easter Seals, the association collecting donations to aide medical research into diseases crippling children.

The longest running has been the annual Muscular Dystrophy Association Labor Day Telethon. It was hosted for many years by Jerry Lewis, who invited the biggest stars to appear. One momentous entertainment event occurred on 1976 MDA telethon, when Frank Sinatra brought a friend to see Jerry and perform. It was Dean Martin, who was Jerry's former show business partner, and this appearance marked the reunion of Martin and Lewis after a 20-year hiatus.

After terrorist attacks in the U.S. on Sept. 11, 2001, a telethon benefiting families of victims of New York City terrorist attacks was simulcast on most networks. "America: A Tribute to Heroes," aired Sept. 21, 2001, and starred Muhammad Ali, Bruce Springsteen, Jack Nicholson, Al Pacino, Goldie Hawn, Kurt Russell, George Clooney, Stevie Wonder, Robin Williams, Clint Eastwood, Julia Roberts, Tom Cruise, Paul Simon, Tom Hanks, Willie Nelson, Kelsey Grammer, The Dixie Chicks, Cameron Diaz, Dennis Franz, Sela Ward, Tom Petty, Bon Jovi, Faith Hill, Jim Carrey, Robert DeNiro, Billy Joel, Ray Romano, Neil Young, Amy Brenneman, Conan O'Brien and Sheryl Crow.

Following Hurricane Katrina, "The Concert for Hurricane Relief" was telecast on Sept. 2, 2005. Viewers were encouraged to donate to the Red Cross Disaster Relief Fund. It was hosted by Matt Lauer and featured such entertainers as Harry Connick Jr., Leonardo DiCaprio, Richard Gere, Tim McGraw, Faith Hill, Aaron Neville, Jimmy Smits and Hilary Swank.

Hurricane Sandy hit New Jersey in late October 2012. "Hurricane Sandy: Coming Together" was a telethon for disaster relief, broadcast on Nov. 2, 2012. Performers included Bruce Springsteen, Billy Joel, Aerosmith, Jon Bon Jovi, Christine Aguilera, Sting, Jon Stewart, Jimmy Fallon and Kevin Bacon.

The music industry has produced many records where the proceeds benefited causes. "Bundle Them Up" was a series of fund raising records for WTAE in Pittsburgh, PA. The project bought coasts for children and seniors who could not afford them. Records have been released since 1987.

Irving Berlin wrote the song "God Bless America." It was considered an anthem of national unity during World War II and still is performed today. The signature recording was by Kate Smith in 1939. Berlin donated the royalties of that song in perpetuity to the Boy Scouts of America.

"Homegrown San Diego" was an annual series of record albums produced for charity by KGB, San Diego's rock radio station. Each was comprised solely of local musicians. The albums sold for $1.01, which was KGB's number on the radio dial. 100% of the profits were donated to The United Way. Hundreds of songs were submitted to KGB to be considered, with 12 chosen for each album, all original songs about life in San Diego County, CA.

"International Piano Festival" concerts were sponsored by the United Nations. Record albums of the festivals raised funds to support UN humanitarian aid.

Holidays

Martin Luther King Jr. Day, the third Monday in January, celebrates the birthday of the humanitarian and civil rights leader. Legislation creating MLK Day as a national holiday was signed into law by President Ronald Reagan. States then voted to accept observe it. MLK Day was observed in all 50 states for the first time in 2000.

Valentine's Day is held on February 14. It became associated with romantic love in the 14th Century and evolved into a holiday in the 18th Century. 190 million valentine cards are sent each year in the U.S. (including 20 million e-Valentines).

President's Day, the third Monday in February, is the current name for the former Washington's Birthday. George Washington was the first President of the United States. The act creating Washington's Birthday was passed by Congress in 1879.

Abraham Lincoln was the 16th President of the U.S., presiding during the Civil War. The holiday commemorating his birth was never an official government holiday, though it was celebrated in many states. The Uniform Monday Holiday Act of 1968 joined Washington's and Lincoln's Birthdays as Presidents Day.

Easter is held each spring, during Holy Week. It commemorates the resurrection of Christ. Easter eggs symbolize the empty tomb of Jesus. The decorating of eggs goes back to the pre-dynastic period in Egypt. The Easter Bunny is a folk symbol, dating back to 1682, where the hare delivered Easter eggs to children. The first chocolate Easter egg was introduced in 1873.

Memorial Day honors those who died while serving in the nation's armed forces. It is observed the last Monday in May. It began as Decoration Day in 1868 and was changed to Memorial Day in 1882. Many visit memorials and cemeteries, laying wreaths and paying tribute to fallen heroes. In 1966, President Lyndon B. Johnson signed a proclamation which declared Waterloo, NY, as the birthplace of Memorial Day. In 2000, Congress passed the National Moment of Remembrance Act, asking people to stop and pay tribute at 3:00 p.m. on Memorial Day.

Independence Day is celebrated on July 4th each year. It commemorates the adoption of the Declaration of Independence on July 4, 1776. The Liberty Bell rang for the second Continental Congress. The first informal celebration was in 1777. The first Independence Day celebration was held in 1796. "America (My Country Tis of Thee)" was first sung in Boston on July 4, 1831. The Statue of Liberty was presented to the U.S. in Paris on July 4, 1884. The U.S. Centennial was held on July 4, 1876, with the Bicentennial on July 4, 1976.

Labor Day is celebrated the first Monday in September, honoring workers and their contributions toward the prosperity of the country. Oregon became the first state to make it a holiday in 1887. It became a federal holiday in 1894. Memorial Day is considered the beginning of summer, and Labor Day marks the end of summer.

Columbus Day is celebrated in October in honor of Christopher Columbus, who discovered America. In the 15th Century, trade and business levels rose. Merchants began traveling from town to town to take orders, place goods and move goods. Craft guilds emerged, as cities became viable customers. Improved transportation stimulated the growth of port cities. The Spanish, Portuguese, French and English began to search for additional trade in Africa, the Middle East and the New World. The merchants accrued sources of wealth, becoming economic and political influencers.

Christopher Columbus crossed the Atlantic and discovered the New World. Explorers were considered the first entrepreneurs, including Hernando de Soto and Francisco Pizzarro. French exploration affected the development of business history because of its heightened scales and affects on governments. Jean-Baptiste Colbert envisioned the roles of merchants and trade as essential to dominating society. Port cities on the Great Lakes and Gulf of Mexico became funnels to exploring the New World and merchant capitalism.

San Francisco started the first Columbus Day parade in 1868. Columbus Day became a state holiday in Colorado in 1906. It became an official U.S. holiday in 1937.

Veteran's Day is observed on November 11 and celebrates the service of all military men and women, current and past. It began with an address by President Woodrow Wilson on Nov. 11, 1919. Congress made Armistice Day a holiday in 1926. The name was changed to Veterans Day in 1954.

Thanksgiving is celebrated the fourth Thursday in November, where citizens give thanks for their blessings. Its heritage goes back to the Protestant Reformation. The English began celebrating it in 1536. Thanksgiving in the U.S. began in 1621 with the feast attended by the pilgrims and native Americans. The custom of holding an annual harvest began in the 1660s.

Christmas is observed on December 25 and celebrates the birth of Jesus Christ. It is a public holiday in many countries and represents a season of celebration by families, friends and communities. The holiday feast is often called "midwinter." The terms "noel" and "nativity" represent the birth of Jesus.

New Year's Day is observed on January 1 and represents celebrations of the old and the expectation of excitingly new beginnings. The chiming of midnight in each time zone signifies the party spirit of the fresh new year ahead. It was first celebrated on Jan. 1, 153 B.C. in Rome. By the 7th Century, the custom of giving gifts was adopted. Jan. 1 was adopted as New Year's Day in Western Europe in 1752. In the 20th Century, New Year's Eve became institutionalized as the night of parties. In the U.S., it is traditional to spend time with loved ones, celebrating good fortune and what lies ahead.

Anniversaries Honor the Past and Build Support for the Future

Anniversaries are important milestones. Organizations reflect on their heritage and accomplishments. In doing so, they build and widen stakeholder bases, enabling organizations to grow for the future.

I've recommended anniversary celebrations to client companies before. In each case, the results were phenomenal, because they took the effort to mount anniversary celebrations. In 1978, I was advising Uniroyal Tire Company. They wanted to sponsor a 40th anniversary for Little League Baseball. My research revealed that their company had in fact founded LLB, which younger generations of management did not know.

In 1998, I advised the Disney corporation and reminded them that Walt Disney's 100th birthday in 2001 would offer great marketing and positioning opportunities. In 2007, I was advising the credit union industry of America, reminding them that their upcoming 100th anniversary in 2009 would provide outreach opportunities for chapter members around the country. This was news to them, and they jumped on it with relish. I'm the person who planted the ideas and strategy. Great organizations work tirelessly to celebrate and involve their customers.

When one reflects at changes, he-she sees directions for the future. Change is innovative. Customs come and go...some should pass and others might well have stayed with us. The past is an excellent barometer for the future. One can always learn from the past, dust it off and reapply it. Living in the past is not good, nor is living in the present without wisdom of the past.

Here are some recent celebrations worthy of acclaim and participation: Civil Rights Act, 50th. Beatles coming to America, 50th. "The Star Spangled Banner" by Francis Scott Key, 200th. "Alice in Wonderland" by Lewis Carroll, 150th. Star Trek, 50th. Sir Isaac Newton discovering gravity, 350th. Launching of the world's first satellite, Sputnik, 60th. "Frankenstein" by Mary Shelley, 200th. NASA lunar landing, 50th. Suez Canal, 150th.

There are seven kinds of anniversary reunions:

1. Pleasurable. Seeing an old friend who has done well, moved in a new direction and is genuinely happy to see you too. These include chance meetings, reasons to reconnect and a concerted effort by one party to stay in the loop.

2. Painful. Talking to someone who has not moved forward. It's like the conversation you had with them 15 years ago simply resumed. They talk only about past matters and don't want to hear what you're doing now. These include people with whom you once worked, old romances, former neighbors and networkers who keep turning up like bad pennies and colleagues from another day and time.

3. Mandated. Meetings, receptions, etc. Sometimes, they're pleasurable, such as retirement parties, open houses, community service functions. Other times, they're painful, such as funerals or attending a bankruptcy creditors' meeting.

4. Instructional. See what has progressed and who have changed. Hear the success stories. High school reunions fit into this category, their value depending upon the mindset you take with you to the occasion.

5. Reflect Upon the Past. Reconnecting with old friends, former colleagues and citizens for whom you have great respect. This is an

excellent way to share each other's progress and give understanding for courses of choice.

6. Benchmarking. Good opportunities to compare successes, case studies, methodologies, learning curves and insights. When "the best" connects with "the best," this is highly energizing.

7. Goal Inspiring. The synergy of your present and theirs inspires the future. Good thinkers are rare. Stay in contact with those whom you know, admire and respect. It will benefit all involved.

7 Levels of Learning from the Past:

1. Re-reading, reviewing and finding new nuggets in old files.
2. Applying pop culture to today.
3. Review case studies and their patterns for repeating themselves.
4. Discern the differences between trends and fads.
5. Learn from successes and three times more from failures.
6. Transition your focus from information to knowledge.
7. Apply thinking processes to be truly innovative.

When we see how far we have come, it gives further direction for the future. Ideas make the future happen. Technology is but one tool of the trade. Futurism is about people, ideas and societal evolution, not fads and gimmicks. The marketplace tells us what they want, if we listen carefully. We also have an obligation to give them what they need.

Apply history to yourself. The past repeats itself. History is not something boring that you once studied in school. It tracks both vision and blind spots for human beings. History can be a wise mentor and help you to avoid making critical mistakes.

The United Nations, the Police Athletic League and Scouting programs.

Smokey the Bear.

Top stars performed on records raising money for worthwhile causes.

Chapter 7

FUND RAISING

Development is a process that utilizes the management tools of analysis, planning, execution, control and evaluation.

The components of development programs include:

- Donor campaigns and programs.
- Grant applications and grant writing.
- Auctions, sales and fairs.
- Consultation from fundraising experts.
- Annual giving.
- Legacies and sponsorships.
- Stewardship and investment.
- Providing public benefit and ethical accountability.

There are several types of non-profit fundraising activities, as listed below.

Annual Fundraising. There is a beginning and an end, during which unrestricted donations are sought. There is a regular set of donors to approach.

There are mostly individuals, including board members, special circle of friends and influential people who are approached for donations. The activity can be organized every year with the same group of people and with the same method, saving time and money, and it is generally effective.

Corporate and Business Fundraising. Most businesses give donations for specific purposes. It also helps with their corporate image and their commitments toward Corporate Social Responsibility. Companies must conduct research to find which organizations to give money and for what types of projects. This process in non-profit fundraising takes time to pursue. The companies take time to process requests, but once accepted, it can be substantial and for a longer period of time.

National and International Government Grants. Several government entities have allocated money for certain causes. It requires research to find and match project goals with theirs. These grants cover certain periods of time. If a charity wins one grant, there is a high probability they will win in consecutive years.

Cause Related Marketing. Some businesses work with non-profit organizations by providing them product sales commissions. The charity organization gets donations in proportion to the sales of certain products. Such funding is influenced by the volume of sales. Through this process, the non-profit fundraising organization also gets some publicity through the media campaigns of the commercial company.

Unrelated Business Income. This results when a non-profit organization acquires a property and runs it as a business to turn it into a fund to run its activities. This activity ensures long-term financial backing. Such companies pay taxes and run their charity activities through the profit achieved by the business. Organizations possessing leaders with business skills can benefit from such fundraising activity.

Planned Giving. Many organizations undertake fundraising as part of the planned giving process. In this program, donors pledge to give certain amounts of money on specific events, such as birthdays, anniversaries and other life events.

Web based portals and software programs enable individuals and organizations to conduct fundraising for social good causes. Sites such as CauseVox, Crowdrise, DonateNow, DonorPerfect, DonorsChoose, FirstGiving,

FunRazr, GiveForward, Givelet, Givezooks, GoFundMe, JustGive, Qgiv, Razoo, StayClassy and YouCaring provide services for individual fundraising, crowd funding and peer-to-peer fundraising.

Crucial to effective fundraising is the care and cultivation of donors, plus the donors' ability to give. Donors must be educated and realize the results of their contributions. Donors must understand the organizations mission and goals, in order to continue their support. The appeal is to the heart and the head.

Organizations move forward if they have solid bases of donors and other advocates. It is more efficient to have long-term relationships with donors, having them take ownership in programs. Still other advocates must be developed through other areas than just fundraising. Cultivating clients and stakeholders as donors means they will take ownership in the outcomes.

Organizations must analyze when they are ready for fundraising. They must examine resources available and donor bases that the competition may already be tapping. Analyze the distribution of gifts, achievable dollar levels and potential sources of grants.

Planning reflects the analysis, addresses the risks, codifies the research and judiciously moves forward with a fundraising strategy. This process allows non-profit organizations to take advantage of opportunities in line with their purpose, service offerings and commitment to their defined publics. Planning will address numbers of gifts needed, dollar levels and how cases of support will be articulated. The planning gift chart helps non-profit leaders understand the potential of the donor base. Planners determine the feasibility of goals by determining the prospects for each gift level.

Execution requires a plan to carry out. Tasks and responsibilities are assigned, with expected standards of accountability. This requires commitment from everyone who will be involved in the program.

Control involves the systems and processes involved. This takes the form of monitoring, coordination, reports, timelines, budgets, leadership and people skills.

Evaluation looks at the targets achieved and missed, determining room for improvement. This objective evaluation determines how resources were managed, constituents; needs being served and whether this campaign contributed to the organization's mission. It involves leadership, staff, volunteers and donors. Evaluation becomes the analysis phase for the next fundraising campaign.

Stakeholders

Everyone needs friends to support their initiatives. Especially when things get tough, it's nice to have constituencies to count upon.

Companies must bank support. Times to call for endorsements inevitably arise. The time to build bridges is today, not when a crisis strikes.

In selling goods and services, third party support may include past and present clients, suppliers and industries affected by your customers.

In affecting policies and disposition toward your doing business, liaisons must be established with elected officials, the judiciary, regulatory agencies, the public sector, advocate groups and private sector opinion makers.

Most companies realize the impact of special-publics support, including various socio-economic and ethnic groups. Cause-related marketing, environmental sensitivity and meaningful "giving back to the community" are essential for the coming years.

Stakeholder Management is an important discipline that successful people use to win support from others. It helps them ensure that their projects succeed where others fail.

Stakeholder Analysis is the technique used to identify the key people who have to be won over. You then use Stakeholder Planning to build the support that helps you succeed.

The benefits of using a stakeholder-based approach are to:

- Use opinions of the most powerful stakeholders to shape your projects at an early stage. Not only does this make it more likely that they will support you, their input can also improve the quality of your project.
- Gain support from powerful stakeholders can help you to win more resources. This makes it more likely that your projects will be successful.
- Assure that they fully understand what you are doing and understand the benefits of your project. This means they can support you actively when necessary.

- Anticipate what people's reaction to your project may be.
- Build into your plan the actions that will win people's support.
- These recommendations are offered in a Stakeholder Program for gaining and maintaining third party support of business initiatives:
- Make lists of your company's current friends and enemies. Update them regularly.
- Determine why friends support you…and what would happen if their backing was lost.
- Understand why some people and groups oppose you. Ascertain what would have prevented their objections and what it would take to turn them around.
- List whom you want to win as friends and with whom you are most afraid of becoming enemies.
- Analyze what your competitors are doing to win friends and build coalitions.
- Foresee what would happen if you sat still and did nothing.
- Project the financial and other benefits of pro-active building of credible third party endorsements.
- Make this initiative a primary responsibility for top management.
- Retain outside counsel with demonstrated expertise in fundraising, community relations, cause-related marketing, minority relations, government relations and grassroots constituency building.

Third party support can move mountains when you need it the most…or it can wreak havoc on your bottom line and the future in which you do business. Be honest about your current status. Take stock of opportunities. Make decisive actions, and reap future rewards.

Stages in Stakeholder Development

1. Identifying Your Stakeholders. The first step is to ascertain who your stakeholders are. Think of all the people who are affected by your work, who have influence or power over it, or have an interest in its

successful or unsuccessful conclusion. Some of the people who might be stakeholders in your job or in your projects include:

- Employees.
- Alliance partners.
- Trade and professional associations.
- Supply chain members, including subcontractors and suppliers: impact on supply costs and deliverability.
- Opinion leaders.
- Regulators and government agencies.
- Financial institutions.
- Advocate groups and special interest groups.
- The media.
- Future recruits and communities in which we would like to expand.

Although stakeholders may be both organizations and people, ultimately you must communicate with people. Make sure that you identify the correct individual stakeholders within a stakeholder organization.

2. Prioritize Your Stakeholders. You may have a list of people and organizations that are affected by your work. Some of these may have the power either to block or advance initiatives. Some may be interested in what you are doing. Map your stakeholders, and classify them by their power over and interest in your work. Someone's position on the grid shows you the actions you have to take with them:

- High power, interested people. These are the people you must fully engage and make the greatest efforts to satisfy.
- High power, less interested people. Put enough work in with these people to keep them satisfied, but not so much that they become bored with your message.
- Low power, interested people. Keep these people adequately informed, and talk to them to assure that no major issues are

arising. These people can often be very helpful with the detail of your project.

- Low power, less interested people. Monitor these people, but do not bore them with excessive communication.

3. Understanding Key Stakeholders. You need to know how they are likely to feel about and react to your project. You also need to know how best to engage them in your project and how best to communicate with them. Key questions that can help you understand your stakeholders are:

- What financial or emotional interest do they have in the outcome of your work? Is it positive or negative?
- What motivates them most of all?
- What information do they want or need from you? How do they want to receive information from you? What is the best way of communicating your message to them?
- What is their current opinion of your work? Is it based on good information?
- Who influences their opinions generally, and who influences their opinion of you? Do some of these influencers therefore become important stakeholders in their own right?
- If they are not likely to be positive, what will win them around to support your project?
- If you don't think you will be able to win them around, how will you manage their opposition?
- Who else might be influenced by their opinions? Do these people become stakeholders in their own right?

A very good way to answer these questions is to talk to your stakeholders directly. People are often quite open about their views, and asking people's opinions is often the first step in building a successful relationship with them.

Stakeholders, as used here, refers to our primary reference groups, those who contribute regularly to our "vocabulary of meaning." Summarize the understanding you have gained, so that you can easily see which stakeholders are expected to be blockers or critics, and which stakeholders are likely to be advocates and supporters or your project.

4. Stages of Stakeholder Involvement include identification, development, monitoring, influencing and involvement. In recent years, a wider variety of goals have been suggested for a business. These include the traditional objective of profit maximization. They also include goals relating to earnings per share, total sales, numbers employed, measures of employee welfare, manager satisfaction, environmental protection and many others.

A major reason for increasing adoption of a Stakeholder Concept in setting business objectives is the recognition that businesses are affected by the "environment" in which they operate. The stakeholder concept suggests that the managers of a business should take into account their responsibilities to other groups and not just the shareholder group, when making decisions. The concept suggests that businesses can benefit significantly from cooperating with stakeholder groups, incorporating their needs in the decision-making process.

Stakeholder programs have the potential to transform the quality of business life. Their main strength is in combination with an appropriate business philosophy, which does not yet exist. Widely respected business values can be identified, but they need to be founded on basic principles, which is a requirement for any discipline to move from ideology to maturity.

5. Roles for stakeholders include:
   • Serve as a Design Team Member: A diverse group of people who are highly invested in this work and who provide a critical perspective by engaging throughout the entire planning process. Their time commitment is the largest. They are the key collaborators on what will be included in the plan drafts. Design teams are often composed of 5-10 people, representing different stakeholder groups. They also

are asked to consider perspectives other than their own or those of the stakeholder group(s) of which they are a part.

- Provide Input: Which stakeholder groups should be asked for their input at various points in the process? Who could have critical insight, experience, or information that can be incorporated into the process? Who will be most impacted by the strategic plan? One strategy for gathering input is to utilize existing meetings (e.g. community partner forums, faculty curriculum committees, staff meetings, student organization meetings) to gather input on their visions for community engagement, or what they perceive to be the greatest barriers or opportunities for strengthening community engagement in higher education.

- Provide Feedback: Who should read drafts of the full plan or portions of it, and provide feedback?

- Approve the Plan: Who needs to formally approve the plan? Who needs to informally approve of the plan because their support is critical?

- Disseminate the Plan: Who should receive a copy of the final plan?

- Other: Are there other processes in which stakeholders should be involved?

Chapter 8

PUTTING ON SPECIAL EVENTS

E vents are plentiful in the non-profit world. Some are special. Others are carbon copies. Still others fail to hit the mark. Planning and strategy are essential to make the event special, memorable, effective and profitable. Here are questions to consider in mounting special events:

1. How will this contribute to the accomplishment of the organization's overall objectives?
2. Who will attend?
3. Who will communicate the organization's messages?
4. What is the message to be communicated through events?
5. How can you make the setting convenient and appealing?
6. Is it worth the time and expense involved?
7. How should attendees feel about your organization as a result of participating?
8. How can these effects be spread to additional audiences?
9. How can you reach those who were invited but did not attend?

10. How much will this cost?

11. Do you have enough time to do it the right way?

12. Do you have the best team available to pull it off?

13. What is your goal? How will you know when you reach it?

14. Is the event mission driven?

15. How does this tie in with other fund raising activities?

16. What public awareness purposes are being served?

17. How can your organization thank stakeholders and build long-lasting bases of support?

In answering these questions, take the perspective of each person involved. If you were they, what would you like to see happen each hour during the event and during the aftermath. Planning and strategies are crucial to successful events.

When you go through this exercise, you will have the details of each event better understood. You'll know what is going to happen, who is responsible, when tasks need to be completed, how much it will cost and where you stand with each activity. Update the status column regularly, and distribute agendas and updates. Follow the progress of people who are charged with each work product, and this will assure things happening as they should.

With good intentions, checklists, strategies and accountabilities, you can predict things that might go wrong and avoid the crises.

Follow this event management checklist:

Pre-planning looks at objectives, audiences, activities, costs, location and logistics.

Having the best committee makes the difference. Select chairs, task coordinators and support staff with common vision and the skills to make your best ideas into realities.

Realize that volunteers will need to be recruited, per tasks and areas of expertise. Staff up, and retain those volunteers, in order to go the distance. Thank volunteers, and keep them motivated.

Make good decisions, and be prepared to justify them. Many events failed because good ideas were not tested.

Invitations may include printed forms, electronic solicitations, reminders by telephone, follow-up mailings and RSVP mechanisms.

Facets of the event will include the program, entertainment participants, honoraria for payment, equipment needed, scripts, housing, transportation, hospitality and mementos.

Facilities dynamics include the number of people to be accommodated, buildings and rooms needed, table requirements, food service, parking and signage.

Equipment needs may include stages, lecterns and podiums, audio-visual equipment, platforms, screens, trade show booths, tables and security devices.

Publicity and promotion should factor prospect lists, promotional mailings, posters, flyers, advertising, media contacts, press kits, photography and video.

Food and beverage consideration should be given to menus, caterers, schedules, staffing, signage, seating, hospitality room service, tables and crowd control.

Printed programs are usually required. Pay attention to content, design, information on the benefiting charity, lists of officers and committees, lists of contributors, design, printing and distribution.

Registration at events must be systematic and includes such elements as registration forms, bank accounts, credit card processing, a reporting system, registration confirmation, host identification, signs and on-site necessities such as tables, chairs, computers, personnel, cash receipts, name badges, pre-registration list and ticket sales.

Transportation must be planned for moving equipment, charter vehicles, parking shuttles, intra-location movement, moving entertainers, transporting VIPs, signage and logistics details.

Escorts and guides are usually needed for special events, accommodating entertainers, speakers, special guests, exhibitors and aboard buses as needed.

Décor considerations include the theme for the event, design elements, entrances and exits, platforms, head tables, dining tables, exhibits and the hospitality suite.

Ticketing is an important facet, including prices, advance sales, printing, distribution, sales reports, ticket and money control, complimentary tickets, press tickets, sales at the doors and collection of tickets at events.

Additional considerations to be included in the planning and strategy include bad weather contingency, exhibits and displays, silent auctions, set-sale tables, entertainment, security, technicians for equipment, ambulance on standby, police, traffic control and valet parking.

The planner must describe the event, principal responsibilities, budget, deadlines and status update procedures. Plan for crises, and have the ability to shift gears as need be.

Charities are ranked and compared with each other. Events must be creative and fun. They must also make money and show good stewardship of resources. The community must be given reasons for engagement. With so many worthy causes and opportunities for support, your event and the cause it represents must stand out. Your event must have the staying power of being repeated in the future.

Meetings, Seminars and Conferences

Meetings, seminars, conferences and retreats are mainstays of business. Many fail to achieve goals because they are not unique. Thus, folks are highly selective about those they will attend.

Here are some tips for organizing and executing successful seminars:

- Have a reasonable business goal for hosting a program. Someone's ego or a half-baked idea will not suffice.
- Designate one company seminar coordinator, with outside demonstrated conference expertise.
- Select the date, time and topics that will most likely spur interest from potential attendees.
- Select a venue that is original and which will inspire creative thought and maximum participation.
- Have attendee prospects in mind, with a plan of how to obtain their addresses.

- Tailor the concept to make it memorable. Remember the most boring seminars that you have previously attended and the great ones. Learn from your past experiences.
- Pick speakers with flair, not those who will bury their heads in speech texts.
- Achieve a good mix of podium speakers and panels, depending upon the subject matter.
- Do not hold your seminar with expectations of media coverage. Your topic must be highly provocative to get the reporters out. However, your business mentor can often disseminate significant highlights of the program afterwards.
- Invitations should clearly state the benefits of attending. In your quest to be creative, do not blur the business goal.
- Thank attendees for coming. Publicly acknowledge members of your staff who did the legwork in orchestrating the meeting.
- Provide handouts. Distribute evaluation forms, yielding ideas for subsequent programs.
- Offer additional information or some other reason for attendees to call you back and to do business with you.

Whether you occasionally sponsor seminars for business development or lend your name to someone else's program, please pay attention that proper thought is applied. Make yourself that rare company that is credited with staging seminars the right way. People will remember your successes, as well as your mistakes.

Every top professional is called upon to speak at some occasion. Networking breakfasts, business clubs, media opportunities, company presentations, prospect meetings and professional development seminars offer opportunities to position your company.

Overcoming the fear of audiences and lack of formal speech training is a hurdle that most executives must accomplish. Some corporate officials make a priority out of seeking high-profile speaking platforms. Somewhere in between lies the ongoing need for public presentations.

A few tips to keep in mind:

- Confirm all speaking engagements in writing.
- If the organization has a newsletter or other advance communications, be sure that your topic and bio are received in time for publication deadlines.
- Send the person who will introduce you a typed one-minute introduction. Don't send a vita and expect him/her to ferret out the pertinent facts. A proper introduction will set the tone for your remarks.
- Understand what you are there to achieve. Leave the engagement with something tangibly gleaned.
- If the talk will be reported in a subsequent newsletter or will be covered by the media, provide an outline, speech text or press release.
- Follow-up correspondence is always in order.
- If public speaking is an expected part of your management position, seek professional speech and media training.
- Employ a marketing advisor with the skills in procuring and scheduling appropriate speaking platforms, as well as the publicity expertise.

Speakers bureaus are important communications tools for major corporations and community organizations alike. You are competing with many good speakers and must treasure those forums that properly showcase you, your ideas and your company's point of view.

Formulate public speaking, seminars and presentations into your company's formal public relations program. Seek more and better platforms each year. Utilize audiences for third party support building. Get newsletter and press coverage, when appropriate.

Special campaigns: war bonds (U.S. Savings bonds), Easter Seals, Girl Scout Cookies, Christmas Seals and supporting the military troops.

Non-Profit Memorabilia. The stuffed bear is from Habitat for Humanity. The glasses commemorate NASA's Apollo 11 moon flight. The paperweight is an award for service from Boy Scouts of America. The CD is from NPR's "Car Talk" radio show. The coffee cups are from United Way and Rotary International. The poster promotes the Shrine Circus.

Chapter 9

COMMUNITY RELATIONS FOR CORPORATIONS, BUSINESSES AND ORGANIZATIONS

Thoughtfulness Pays Dividends

For those doing business on a long-term basis, respect and understanding of the company will improve its chances. No matter the size of the organization, goodwill must be banked. Every company must make deposits for those inevitable times in which withdrawals will be made.

To say that business and its communities do not affect each other, is short-sighted and will make business the loser every time. Communities surround business but are not subject to its policies and operations. While business usually caters to its own agenda, the community is flexible, unpredictable and emotional.

When business practices and performance pose potential harm to the community, an expected backlash will occur. Communities used to be passive because company presence meant jobs and economic incentive. The mobility of business has forced communities to compete for other businesses, which makes them very Leary of companies that defy the public's best interests.

Since one cannot market a problem-ridden culture, the communities are addressing the troubles, in order to attract more responsible organizations. In this era, the community has spoken out. Business is on fair notice to get its act together.

Communities are clusters of individuals, each with its own agenda. In order to be minimally successful, business must know the components of its community intimately.

No company can cure community problems by itself, unless it is the problem. But each company has a business stake for doing its part. Community relations is a function of self-interest, rather than just being a good citizen.

No company can deal with all components of a community or take on all the problems. The art is to identify those constituencies who serve or can harm the company's strongest needs.

To prioritize which spheres or causes to serve, business should list and examine all of the community's problems. Relate business responses to real and perceived wants/needs of the community. Set priorities.

The only constraints upon community relations are regulatory standards and the amount of resources that can be allocated. There can never be a restraint upon creativity.

Every community relations program has five steps:

1. Learn what each community thinks about the company and, therefore, what information needs to be communicated to each public. Conduct focus groups. Maintain community files. Organize an ongoing feedback system.
2. Plan how to best reach each public and which avenues will be the most expedient. Professional strategic planning counsel performs an independent audit and guides the company through the process. Get as many ideas from qualified sources as possible. Find compatible causes to champion. Maintain contingency plans.
3. Develop systems to execute the program, communicating at every step to publics. All employees should have access to the plan, with a mechanism

that allows them to contribute. If others understand what the company is doing, they will want to be part of it.

4. Evaluate how well each program and its messages were received. Continue fact-finding efforts, which will yield more good ideas for future projects. Document the findings. Build into all community relations programs some realistic mechanisms by which results can be shown. When planning, reach for feasible evaluation yardsticks.

5. Interpret the results to management in terms that are easy to understand and support. Community relations is difficult to evaluate, unless a procedure for doing so is set. Provide management with information that justifies their confidence. Squarely address goals and concerns.

Companies should support off-duty involvement of employees in pro bono capacities but not take unfair credit. Volunteers are essential to community relations. Companies must show tangible evidence of supporting the community by assigning key executives to high-profile community assignments. Create a formal volunteer guild, and allow employees the latitude and creativity to contribute to the common good. Celebrate and reward their efforts.

Community Relations and Cause Related Marketing Are Business Strategies, Not Sales Promotions.

Business marries the community that it settles with. The community has to be given a reason to care for the business. Business owes its well-being and livelihood to its communities.

I recently stopped for lunch at a franchise restaurant. Nobody was at the register. A crew member told me to wait, then later took my order. She started selling donations to some cause, which I declined. When the regular cashier returned, I saw her peddling donation sales. People were blindly making donations, without understanding what they supported. The sales of those promotional pieces caused the line to grow out of the restaurant door. People were just buying the promotion in order to get through the line.

I support cause related marketing and have advised many corporations on setting up such programs. However, peddling sales to some "foundation" that is named after your product and which supports only one cause is not appropriate. The store was littered with stickers. The process of selling the stickers made the waiting line longer. As a result, the iced tea had run out, and nobody checked it.

I went to their website, where franchise chains allege they want customer comments. I stated, "Having a foundation to support the community across the board is great. Who is to say that a sales promotion tied directly to your products is right? I say it is not, and I'm an expert on cause-related marketing. You need to revise your service lines. Peddling the sales of stickers in a tackily littered store is inappropriate. I'm gravely concerned about this practice of badgering customers in support of some phantom charity; how this store does it is not right."

The franchise owner later called. He talked all over me in a defensive manner. His voice was high-pressure, probably the result of sales training classes. Rather than addressing my concerns, he rifled over them and questioned my ability to assess community relations. I asked if he had ever heard of Thousand Points of Light. He said no. I explained what it was and that I was an adviser to the President of the United States in fostering the program. Still, he questioned my interest in community relations.

"We're a franchise," he admitted. "This was dictated to us by corporate. I'm sorry that you feel that way because we do so much good. You're invited to attend when we present the donation." I replied, "No, I'm not going to be a prop in your photo opportunity, for you to sell product." I reminded him that it was customer donations that enabled the attention, not a corporate initiative for which they were taking the credit.

He was not listening. He was simply rationalizing a corporate marketing initiative. So too was the corporate person who later called to argue with me for daring to state my opinions. Sadly, people like that don't care or even get that re-thinking their strategy is an option.

There are many wonderful ways where companies support the community:

- Give percentages of sales to approved charities.
- Offer certificates for product when people make legitimate donations.

- Coupon book activities with schools.
- Allow non-profit groups to present on their premises.
- Advocate community causes in their advertising.
- Sponsor noteworthy community events.
- Recognize that executive time spent in the community is good for business.

No company can cure community problems by itself. Each company has a business stake for doing its part. To prioritize which spheres or causes to serve, business should list and examine all of the community's problems. Relate business responses to real and perceived wants/needs of the community. Set priorities. There can never be a restraint upon creativity.

My advice to companies as they create charity tie-in, cause-related marketing and community relations activities includes:

- Don't say that you want customer input unless you are prepared to really hear it.
- Franchisers should not sell sure-fire promotions to build sales as part of the worth of the franchise.
- Community support is not a one-cause vested-interest matter.
- If you seek customer comment, do not talk over the customer.
- Do not keep rationalizing flawed strategies to your customers.
- Realize that customers' opinions matter and that they have more buying choices than just your store.
- If you purport to have a foundation, it cannot or should not be named directly for your product.
- Do not run your "foundation" out of a corporate marketing department.

Determining the Right Kind of Tie-In Causes
Every community relations program has five steps:

1. Learn what each community thinks about the company and, therefore, what information needs to be communicated to each public. Conduct

focus groups. Maintain community files. Organize an ongoing feedback system.

2. Plan how to best reach each public…which avenues will be the most expedient. Professional strategic planning counsel performs an independent audit and guides the company through the process. Get as many ideas from qualified sources as possible.

3. Develop systems to execute the program, communicating at every step to publics. All employees should have access to the plan, with a mechanism that allows them to contribute. If others understand what the company is doing, they will be part of it.

4. Evaluate how well each program and its messages were received. Continue fact-finding efforts, which will yield more good ideas for future projects. Document the findings. When planning, reach for feasible evaluation yardsticks.

5. Interpret the results to management in terms that are easy to understand and support. Provide management with information that justifies their confidence.

Companies should support off-duty involvement of employees in pro-bono capacities but not take unfair credit. Volunteers are essential to community relations. Companies must show tangible evidence of supporting the community. Create a formal volunteer guild, and allow employees the latitude and creativity to contribute to the common good. Celebrate and reward their efforts.

In some cases, corporations would do well to create stand-alone foundations to bring greater cohesion to their giving strategies and community relations activity.

Community relations is action-oriented and should include one or more of these forms:

1. Creating something necessary that did not exist before.
2. Eliminating something that poses a problem.
3. Developing the means for self-determination.
4. Including citizens who are in need.

5. Sharing professional and technical expertise.
6. Tutoring, counseling and training.
7. Promotion of the community to outside constituencies.
8. Moving others toward action.

Publicity and promotions should support community relations and not be the substitute or smokescreen for the process. Recognition is as desirable for the community as for the business. Good news shows progress and encourages others to participate.

The well-rounded community relations program embodies all elements: accessibility of company officials to citizens, participation by the company in business and civic activities, public service promotions, special events, plant communications materials and open houses, grassroots constituency building and good citizenry.

Never stop evaluating. Facts, values, circumstances and community composition are forever changing. The same community relations posture will not last forever. Use research and follow-up techniques to reassess the position, assure continuity and move in a forward motion.

No business can operate without affecting or being affected by its communities. Business must behave like a guest in its communities...never failing to show or return courtesies. Community acceptance for one project does not mean than the job of community relations has completed.

Community relations is not "insurance" that can be bought overnight. It is tied to the bottom line and must be treated accordingly, with resources and expertise to do it effectively. It is a bond of trust that, if violated, will haunt the business. If steadily built, the trust can be exponentially parlayed into successful long-term business relationships.

Chapter 10

CAUSES CHAMPIONED
BY PUBLIC FIGURES

C elebrities are in a position to support and further worthwhile causes. Singers, actors and business leaders become attached to causes along the way. Others remain deeply committed to giving back as a career-long dedication, becoming humanitarians. In all cases, celebrities help to shine the spotlight on issues, which leads to others supporting.

Muhammad Ali was the three-time world heavyweight boxing champion. He invented the expressions "rope a dope" and "float like a butterfly, sting like a bee." He was presented with the Presidential Medal of Freedom in 2005. The non-profit Muhammad Ali Center is located in Louisville, KY. Ali devoted his life to helping promote world peace, civil rights, cross-cultural understanding, interfaith relations, humanitarianism, hunger relief and the commonality of basic human values. Muhammad Ali was honored by Amnesty International, accorded their Lifetime Achievement Award. The Celebrity Fight Night Foundation formed in 1994 and hosts annual charity events in honor of Ali. His other causes include the Ali Care Program, Athletes for Hope, Muhammad Ali Parkinson Center, Project A.L.S., and Special Olympics.

Harry Belafonte is a popular singer, songwriter, actor and won three Grammy Awards, an Emmy Award and a Tony Award. He served the American Civil Liberties Union as celebrity ambassador for juvenile justice issues. In 1989, he received a Kennedy Center Honors award.

Bono was the lead singer of the rock group U2. He has steadfastly fought poverty and hunger and is in direct contact with world leaders and policy makers in his quest to make the world a better place. In 1986 he helped organize Amnesty International's Conspiracy of Hope tour with Sting, Peter Gabriel, Lou Reed and Bryan Adams. World Vision invited Bono to Ethiopia, where he developed an education program that used plays and songs to spread information on health issues. Bono has been a leader in the fight against poverty, and has received three nominations for the Nobel Peace Prize. Other causes he has supported include Amnesty International, the Clinton Global Initiative, Every Mother Counts, the Legacy of Hope Foundation, MusiCares, the NAACP and Zero Hunger.

President George H.W. Bush launched Thousand Points of Light. It recognized citizens and companies for community good deeds and stewardship. It now has 250 affiliates in 22 countries.

James Earl Carter was President of the U.S. from 1977-1981, the only U.S. president who once lived in public assistance housing. He was a peanut farmer and Governor of Georgia prior to becoming President. In 1982, he established the Carter Center as the basis for advancing human rights. He has conducted peace negotiations, has monitored 96 elections in 38 nations and has fostered programs to reduce disease in under-developed nations. He has been a major proponent of Habitat For Humanity. In 2002, he received the Nobel Peace Prize for his work "to find peaceful solutions to international conflicts, to advance democracy and human rights, and to promote economic and social development."

George Clooney is a popular actor and film industry leader. He has raised money to help victims of torture, starvation, homelessness and rights violations. He has supported Realizing the Dream, continuing the work of Dr. and Mrs. Martin Luther King in wiping out poverty and injustice. He was named a United Nations Messenger of Peace in 2008.

Bob Hope (1903-2003) was a major star of radio, TV, movies and concerts. His theme song was "Thanks For the Memory." When the U.S. sent troops into

World War II, Hope toured the bases around the world. His USO tours were equally active during the Korean War, Vietnam, the Persian-Gulf War and times in between. His USO tours over half a century drew other stars to appear and set the tone for other tours by other performers.

Michael Jackson (1958-2009) was a major recording and concert star over four decades. He co-wrote "We Are The World" with Lionel Richie in 1985 and performed it to raise money for Africa in 1985. In 1986, he established the "Michael Jackson United Negro College Fund Endowed Scholarship Fund" ($1.5 million for scholarships to students in performance art and communications). He donated the proceeds from "Man In The Mirror" to Camp Ronald McDonald for Good Times, a camp for children with cancer. He also established ChildHelp USA and the Heal the World Foundation.

Elton John has been a commanding force on music since 1969, with countless hit records, concerts and videos. He established an AIDS Foundation in 1992, inspired by his young friend Ryan White, who died of AIDS in 1990. It has raised $200 million to support HIV/AIDS programs in 55 countries.

Angelina Jolie, Oscar-winning actress, has been a humanitarian spokesperson. Since 2001, she has represented the Office of the United Nations High Commissioner for Refugees (UNHCR), the agency mandated to lead and co-ordinate protection of refugees. On field missions, she met with refugees and internally displaced persons in Sierra Leone, Tanzania, Cambodia, Pakistan, Thailand, Ecuador, Kosovo, Kenya, Namibia, Sri Lanka, North Caucasus, Jordan, Egypt, New Delhi, Costa Rica, Chad, Syria and Iraq. The Jolie-Pitt Foundation addresses rural poverty, protecting natural resources and conserving wildlife. In 2003, Jolie was the first recipient of the Citizen of the World Award from the United Nations Correspondents Association. Jolie has attended World Refugee Day in Washington, D.C. and was a speaker at the World Economic Forum. Jolie co-chaired the Education Partnership for Children of Conflict, which helps fund education programs for children affected by conflict. Jolie published "Notes from My Travels," a collection of journal entries on her field missions, with proceeds benefitting UNHCR.

President John F. Kennedy advocated for the arts. The Kennedy Center for the Performing Arts opened in 1971 and presents theatre, dance, ballet, orchestral, chamber, folk, jazz and pop concerts. It is the busiest performing arts complex in the U.S. A major event is Kennedy Center Honors, held each December.

Norman Lear produced many successful TV series in the 1970s and 1980s, including "All in the Family," "Sanford and Son," "The Jeffersons," "Maude" and "Good Times." In 1981, he founded People for the American Way, advocating human rights and progressive causes.

Jerry Lewis was the personification of the Muscular Dystrophy Association, which was founded in 1950. Lewis hosted its first fund raising telethon, and it has remained an annual event each Labor Day. MDA combats muscular dystrophy and diseases of the nervous system by funding research, treatment and patient education. Lewis got the biggest stars to appear on his annual telethons. One momentous event occurred in 1976 when Frank Sinatra brought a friend to see Jerry and perform. It was Dean Martin, who was Jerry's former show business partner, and this appearance marked the reunion of Martin and Lewis after a 20-year hiatus. MDA telethons were huge, and they inspired other telethons for other causes to follow suit.

Paul McCartney helped organize the Concert For New York City in 2001. He performed at several charity concerts, including the Prince's Trust, Live 8, U.S. Campaign for Burma, Concerts for the People of Kampuchea, Band Aid, Live Aid and the Hillsborough disaster fundraiser. Other causes he has supported included Adopt-A-Minefield, Keep A Child Alive, Make Poverty History, Teenage Cancer Trust, TigerTime, Voices Against Violence and Whatever It Takes.

Marie Osmond and her family founded the Children's Miracle Network Hospitals in Salt Lake City, UT, in 1983, along with John Schneider, Joe Lake and Mick Shannon. It raises funds for 170 children's hospitals in the U.S. and Canada, plus medical research and public education on children's health issues.

Prince Rogers Nelson (1958-2016) had many hit records over 35 years. He won Grammy Awards, a Golden Globe Award and an Oscar for Best Song Score ("Purple Rain"). Prince made many charitable and humanitarian contributions, without seeking public notoriety. He helped create "Yes We Code," having technology companies working with inner-city kids, getting them ready for jobs in Silicon Valley. He supported "Green for All," an environmental initiative and gave millions anonymously.

Princess Diana of Wales (1961-1997) was active in various charities seeking improvements in human welfare, from AIDS to a campaign to prevent landmines. She visited terminally ill people across the world and championed animal welfare programs. Other causes that Princess Diana supported included Help the Aged, the Trust for Sick Children, the youth branch of the British Red Cross, Chester Childbirth Appeal, National Hospital for Neurology and Neurosurgery, Dove House, Meningitis Trust, Welsh National Opera, Preschool Playgroups Association, Royal School for the Blind, Malcolm Sargent Cancer Fund for Children, the Guinness Trust, Birthright, Variety Club, National Children's Orchestra, Royal Brompton Hospital and Eureka.

Franklin D. Roosevelt was the 32nd President of the U.S. He launched the March of Dimes Foundation in 1938 to combat polio. It works to improve the health of mothers and babies.

Sting was born Gordon Matthew Thomas Sumner. As lead vocalist with The Police and a solo artist was named one of the 100 greatest musical stars of the 20th Century. He got involved in human rights activism in 1981 and participated in many causes, including "Conspiracy of Hope," "Band Aid," "Music for Montserrat," "Live Earth," "Hope for Haiti Now," "Human Rights Now" and "Live 8." World leaders have enlisted his counsel on global issues. Sting has been praised for humanitarian service, including the 2014 Kennedy Center Honors.

Elizabeth Taylor was a popular movie star in the 1940s, 1950s, 1960s and 1970s. She is known for such classics as "Cat on a Hot Tin Roof," "National Velvet," "A Place in the Sun," "Father of the Bride," "Giant," "Taming of the Shrew," "Raintree County," "Cleopatra" and "Suddenly Last Summer." She won Oscars for two films, "Butterfield 8" and "Who's Afraid of Virginia Woolf." Elizabeth Taylor was a leader in AIDS activism, including founding the American Foundation for AIDS Research and establishment of the Elizabeth Taylor AIDS Foundation. She was accorded Lifetime Achievement Awards by the American Film Institute, Screen Actors Guild and British Academy of Film and Television

Arts. In 1992, the Academy Awards gave her the Jean Hersholt Humanitarian Award. In 2002, she was given the Kennedy Center Honors award.

Danny Thomas was building a career as a standup comic in the early 1950s. He vowed that when he made it big, he would establish a legacy to children's healthcare. In 1962, Thomas founded St. Jude Children's Research Hospital, a pediatric treatment and research center, in Memphis, TN, with help from Lemuel Diggs and Anthony Abraham. It was named after Thomas' patron saint, St. Jude Thaddeus but is non-denominational and open to all. The institution has advanced successes in cancer treatment, pediatric brain tumor treatment and survival from lymphoblastic leukemia. Danny's daughter Marlo is the national spokesperson for St. Jude's, which opened the Marlo Thomas Center for Global Education and Collaboration in 2014.

Ted Turner became a media mogul by purchasing a UHF station in Atlanta, GA, and beaming it nationally on TV cable systems. WTBS became the flagship of a TV empire that included Cable News Network, TNT, The Cartoon Network and Turner Classic Movies. He owned the Atlanta Braves baseball team. Turner focused on humanitarian activities, establishing the Better World Fund, plus the Goodwill Games. He created the Turner Foundation to focus on environmental and population issues. In 1990, he was named "Humanist of the Year" by the American Humanist Association. In 1991, he was named Time Magazine's "Man of the Year."

Oprah Winfrey hosted a popular syndicated TV talk show from 1986-2011. She was acclaimed for celebrity interviews and entered the publishing industry with "O, The Oprah Magazine." She advocated reading programs, which stimulated the book industry and brought support to literacy programs. In 1998, she created Oprah's Angel Network to muster and disperse resources to non-profit organizations around the world. As a result, more than $80 million was raised. She was awarded the Presidential Medal of Freedom in 2013.

First Ladies of the United States
Dolly Madison championed efforts to help orphans by dressing in elegant fashions.

Eleanor Roosevelt advanced the status of First Lady from hostess at events to that of advocate and leader on public policies. She was known for social activism, championing the plight of the poor. She authored a weekly newspaper column and hosted a radio show. She was a delegate to the United Nations and helped write the Universal Declaration of Human Rights. She championed a variety of non-partisan public works.

Jacqueline Kennedy established the White House Historical Association. Here interest in the arts, culture and historical preservation captured the admiration of the nation.

Lady Bird Johnson pioneered environmental protection and beautification. She created the First Ladies Commission for a More Beautiful Capitol. After the White House, she championed many environmental causes, including Keep America Beautiful. Mrs. Johnson and actress Helen Hayes founded the National Wildflower Research Center in 1982. Her books include "A White House Diary" and "Wildflowers Across America."

Pat Nixon was a strong proponent of volunteerism in community service. She fortified the White House art collection and advocated for many arts groups.

Betty Ford was associated with healthcare advocacy. She advocated for the Equal Rights Amendment. She championed drug and alcohol abuse treatment programs, breast cancer awareness and later founded the Betty Ford Clinic.

Rosalynn Carter worked with the mentally ill, chairing the President's Commission on Mental Health. She continued to lead humanitarian programs for the Carter Center.

Nancy Reagan launched the "Just Say No" campaign, seeking to decrease usage of drugs and alcohol among young people. She later championed stem cell research.

Barbara Bush channeled efforts on the issues of literacy and elder care.

Hillary Clinton chaired the National Commission on Health Care Reform. She advocated for children, authoring the book "It Takes a Village." She was subsequently elected to the U.S. Senate and later served as Secretary of State.

Laura Bush continued the emphasis on literacy. She had formerly worked as a school librarian.

Michelle Obama has championed physical fitness and healthy lifestyles, including leading exercise and wise food choices for children and families. She championed for better education.

Entertainers Who Went Into Public Service

Sonny Bono was a music innovator, as a songwriter, as part of Phil Spector's record production team and as half of Sonny & Cher. His duo had hit records, starred in movies and headlined TV series. Sonny entered business, then was elected to the U.S. Congress.

Jimmie Davis was a singer and songwriter who was inducted into six music halls of fame. He served two terms as Governor of Louisiana, from 1944-1948 and 1960-1964.

Irene Dunne was a popular movie star in the 1930s and 1940s. She is known for such classics as "Love Story," "Show Boat," "Penny Serenade," "The Awful Truth," "Anna and the King of Siam," "Roberta," "A Guy Named Joe," "Stingaree," "My Favorite Wife," "Life With Father" and "White Cliffs of Dover." In the 1950s, she devoted herself to charity work. In 1957, she was appointed as a special U.S. delegate to the United Nations during the 12th General Assembly by President Dwight D. Eisenhower.

Al Franken was a comedian whop served as a writer and performer on "Saturday Night Live" in the 1970s and 1980s. He has served as U.S. Senator from Minnesota since 2009.

John Gavin was an actor, appearing in such films as "Imitation of Life," "Midnight Lace," "Psycho," "Spartacus," "Romanoff and Juliet," "Tammy Tell Me True," "A Breath of Scandal" and "Back Street." From 1961-1965, he was an adviser to the Organization of American States. From 1971-1973, he served as President of the Screen Actors Guild. From 1981-1986, he served as U.S. Ambassador to Mexico.

Fred Grandy appeared as Gopher on the popular TV series "The Love Boat" (1977-1986). He was elected in his home state of Iowa to serve in the U.S. House of Representatives from 1987-1995. He served as President and CEO of Goodwill Industries International from 1995-2000. He later became a political radio commentator and talk show host.

Helen Gahagan was an actress in the 1930s. Walt Disney modeled the queen in "Snow White and the Seven Dwarfs" after her. She was married to actor Melvyn Douglas. She entered into politics in 1940 and served in the U.S. House of Representatives from 1945-51, the first Democratic woman elected to Congress from California.

Dolores Hart was an actress in the 1950s and 1960s. She co-starred with Elvis Presley in two films ("Loving You" and "King Creole"). Other films she appeared in included "Where the Boys Are," "Come Fly With Me," "Wild is the Wind," "Francis of Assisi" and "Lisa." In 1963, she left Hollywood and became a nun. She entered the strictly cloistered Benedictine Regina Laudis Monastery, in Bethlehem, CT. She became Rev. Mother of the Benedictine order, prioress of the Roman Catholic abbey of Regina Laudis, in Bethlehem, CT.

Glenda Jackson was a British actress and member of the Royal Shakespeare Company. She starred in such movies as "Sunday Bloody Sunday," "A Touch of Class," "Women in Love," "Mary, Queen of Scots," "Nasty Habits" and "House Calls." For film work, she won two Academy Awards as Best Actress. From 1992-2010, Jackson served as a member of Parliament in the U.K.

Ben Jones was an actor, best known for playing Cooter Davenport on "The Dukes of Hazzard." He served as a member of the U.S. House of Representatives from 1989-1993, representing Georgia. He runs a chain of Cooter's Museums and the annual Dukefest in tribute to the popular TV series.

John Davis Lodge was the grandson of Senator Henry Cabot Lodge. As an actor, he played Shirley Temple's father in "The Little Colonel." Other films included "Bulldog Drummond at Bay" and "The Scarlet Empress." Representing the state of Connecticut, he served as a member of the U.S. House of Representatives from 1947-51. He served as Governor of Connecticut from 1951-55. Then came diplomatic appointments. Lodge served as U.S. Ambassador to Spain from 1955-61, U.S. Ambassador to Argentina from 1969-73 and U.S. Ambassador to Switzerland from 1983-85.

Clare Boothe Luce started her career as an actress, understudying Mary Pickford on Broadway when she was 10. Clare became interested in the campaign to win the vote for women. In 1935, she married Henry Luce, publisher of Time, Life, Fortune and Sports Illustrated. She authored books and the scripts of films, notably 1939's "The Women." She focused on journalism during World War II. She served in the U.S. Congress from 1943-47, representing Connecticut's 4th district. She was one of the Congressmen who was instrumental in creating the Atomic Energy Commission. She was U.S. Ambassador to Italy from 1953-56 and U.S. Ambassador to Brazil in 1959, both appointments from President Dwight D. Eisenhower. She was awarded the Presidential Medal of Freedom in 1983.

George Murphy was a song and dance man, appearing in such movies as "Broadway Melody of 1938," "Battleground," "Border Incident," "Broadway Melody of 1940," "Step Lively," "Tenth Avenue Angel," "Little Miss Broadway," "This is the Army" and "For Me and My Gal." Murphy was president of the Screen Actors Guild from 1944-46. He was accorded an honorary Academy Award in 1951. He served in the U.S. Senate from 1965-1971. Murphy's move from the screen to California politics paved the way for such other actors as Ronald Reagan and Arnold Schwarzenegger.

W. Lee O'Daniel headed advertising for the Burrus Mill Flower Company in Fort Worth, TX, in the 1920s. He wrote jingles and hired a band to back his vocals. They appeared on the radio as the Light Crust Doughboys. He then formed the Hillbilly Flour Company and put together another band to promote it. He served as Governor of Texas from 1939-1941 and member of the U.S. Senate from 1941-49.

Kal Penn was an actor, appearing in several movies (including the "Harold and Kumar" series) and on the "House" TV show. He then served as Associate Director in the White House Office of Public Engagement for the Barack Obama administration.

Sidney Poitier was a popular movie star in the 1950s, 1960s and 1970s. He is known for such classics as "Lillies of the Field," "A Raisin in the Sun," "A Patch of Blue," "To Sir With Love," "Guess Who's Coming to Dinner," "In the Heat of the Night," "A Piece of the Action" and "Uptown Saturday Night." He later served as Bahamas Ambassador to Japan from 1997-2007. He was an ambassador of the Bahamas to UNESCO from 2002-2007. He was awarded the Presidential Medal of Freedom in 2009.

Ronald Reagan was an actor under contract to Warner Bros. Studios in the 1930s and 1940s, with an impressive list of screen appearances. In the 1950s, he became host of the popular CBS-TV series "General Electric Theatre." He continued appearing in movies and on TV until 1965, when he entered the political arena. Reagan was elected Governor of California in 1966 and President of the United States in 1980.

Arnold Schwarzenegger held the professional body building title Mr. Universe from 1968-1970 and the title Mr. Olympia from 1970-1980. Schwarzenegger starred in hit movies like "Terminator" and "The Running Man." He served as Governor of California from 2003-2011.

Shirley Temple was a child actress, named Hollywood's top box office star from 1935-38. She exemplified movie magic in such films as "Bright Eyes," "The Little Colonel," Little Princess," "Wee Willie Winkie," "Our Little Girl," "Captain January," "Curly Top" and "Heidi." She appeared in films as a teen and adult, headlining her own TV series, "Shirley Temple's Storybook." She is 18th on the American Film Institute's list of screen legends in the classic era. She served as an ambassador to the United Nations General Assembly in 1969, U.S. Ambassador to Ghana (1974-76), U.S. Ambassador to Czechoslovakia (1989-1992) and Chief of Protocol for the U.S. (1976-77). She was Grand Marshal of the New Year's Day Rose Parade in Pasadena, CA, three times (1939, 1989 and 1999).

Fred Thompson was a lawyer from Tennessee, serving as counsel to the Senate Watergate Committee during its hearings in 1973-74. He was counsel to the Senate Foreign Relations Committee (1980-81), the Senate Intelligence Committee (1982). He then appeared as an actor in such movies as "Marie," "No Way Out," "Die Hard 2," "The Hunt for Red October," "Curly Sue," "Class Action," "Cape Fear" and "Days of Thunder." He served in the U.S. Senate from 1994-2003, then returned to acting on the NBC-TV series "Law & Order."

Jesse Ventura had a successful professional wrestling career, known as Jesse "The Body" Ventura. He performed from 1975-1986 and is a member of the World Wrestling Federation Hall of Fame. He then appeared as a commentator on wrestling TV shows. He appeared as an actor in such movies as "Predator," "The Running Man," "Abraxas, Guardian of the Universe," "Batman & Robin,"

"Demolition Man," "Master of Disguise" and "The Ringer. Ventura served as Mayor of Brooklyn Park, MN, from 1991-95 and Governor of Minnesota from 1999-2003.

These stars served as mayors in their communities:

- Alan Autry co-starred in TV series such as "In the Heat of the Night" and "Grace Under Fire." He served as Mayor of Fresno, CA, from 2001-2009.
- Clint Eastwood, film star and director, served as Mayor of Carmel-by-the-Sea, CA, from 1986-88.
- Jack Kelly, best known from ABC-TV's "Maverick" series, served as Mayor of Huntington Beach, CA.
- Ed Nelson, one of the stars of TV's "Peyton Place" series served as Mayor of San Dimas, CA.
- Jerry Springer, reality TV star, served as Mayor of Cincinnati, Ohio.
- Frank Britton Wenzel was a vaudeville performer in the 1920s and 1930s, elected Mayor of Malverne, NY, in 1951.

These actors served as President of the Screen Actors Guild:

- Ralph Morgan, 1933 and 1938-40
- Eddie Cantor, 1933-35
- Robert Montgomery, 1935-38, 1946-47
- Edward Arnold, 1940-42
- James Cagney, 1942-44
- George Murphy, 1944-46
- Ronald Reagan, 1947-52, 1959-60
- Walter Pidgeon, 1952-57
- Leon Ames, 1957-58
- Howard Keel, 1958-59
- George Chandler, 1960-63
- Dana Andrews, 1963-65
- Charlton Heston, 1965-71

- John Gavin, 1971-73
- Dennis Weaver, 1973-75
- Kathleen Nolan, 1975-79
- William Schallert, 1979-81
- Edward Asner, 1981-85
- Patty Duke, 1985-88
- Barry Gordon, 1988-95
- Richard Masur, 1995-99
- William Daniels, 1999-2001
- Melissa Gilbert, 2001-05
- Alan Rosenberg, 2005-09
- Ken Howard, 2009-2016

Sports Figures Who Turned to Public Service

Dave Bing played basketball for the Detroit Pistons, Washington Bullets and Boston Celtics in the NBA from 1966-1978. Since 2009, he has served as Mayor of Detroit, MI.

Bill Bradley played basketball for the New York Knicks in the NBA from 1967-1977. He served in the U.S. Senate from 1979-1997, representing New Jersey.

Jim Bunning played baseball for the Detroit Tigers, Philadelphia Phillies, Pittsburgh Pirates and Los Angeles Dodgers in the MLB from 1955-1971. He served in the U.S. Senate from 1999-2011, representing Kentucky.

Ben Nighthorse Campbell competed in the 1964 Olympics in Judo. He served in the U.S. Senate from 1993-2005, representing Colorado.

Terry Dehere played basketball for the Los Angeles Clippers, Sacramento Kings and Vancouver Grizzlies in the NBA from 1993-1999. He served on the Jersey City Board of Education from 2007-2010.

Kevin Johnson played basketball for the Cleveland Cavaliers and Phoenix Suns in the NBA, from 1987-2000. Since 2008, he has served as Mayor of Sacramento, CA.

Jack Kemp was a professional Quarterback playing for the Pittsburgh Steelers, Calgary Stampeders, L.A./San Diego Chargers and Buffalo Bills in the NFL. He served in the U.S. House of Representatives from 1971-1989, representing New York.

Steve Largent played football for the Seattle Seahawks in the NFL from 1976-1989. He served in the U.S. House of Representatives from 1994-2002, representing Oklahoma.

Don Lash competed in the 1936 Olympics in track and field. He served in the Indiana State House of Representatives from 1973-1982.

Bob Mathias won the gold medals for the decathlon in the 1948 and 1952 Olympic Games. He served in the U.S. House of Representatives from 1967-1975, representing California.

Tom McMillen played basketball for the Buffalo Braves, New York Knicks, Atlanta Hawks and Washington Bullets in the NBA from 1974-1986. He served in the U.S. House of Representatives from 1987-1993, representing Maryland.

Ralph Metcalfe competed in the 1932 and 1936 Olympic Games in Track and Field. He served in the U.S. House of Representatives from 1971-1978, representing Illinois.

Jack Mildren played football for the Baltimore Colts and New England Patriots in the NFL from 1972-1974. He was elected the Lt. Governor of Oklahoma in 1990.

Wilmer David Mizell played baseball for the St. Louis Cardinals, Pittsburgh Pirates and New York Mets in the MLB from 1952-1962. He served in the U.S. House of Representatives from 1969-1975, representing North Carolina.

Tom Osborne played football for the San Francisco 49ers and Washington Redskins in the NFL from 1959-1961. He also served in the U.S. House of Representatives from 2001-2007, representing Nebraska.

Alan Page played football for the Minnesota Vikings and Chicago Bears in the NFL from 1967-1981. He has served as an Associate Justice on the Minnesota Supreme Court since 1993.

Jon Runyan played football for the Houston Oilers, Tennessee Titans, Philadelphia Eagles and San Diego Chargers in the NFL from 1996-2009. He also served in the U.S. House of Representatives since 2011, representing New Jersey.

Ed Rutkowski played football in the American Football League from 1963-1968. He served as deputy commissioner of the New York State Office of Parks, Recreation and Historic Preservation from 1995-2007.

Jim Ryun competed in the 1968 Olympic Games in track and field. He served in the U.S. House of Representatives from 1996-2007, representing Kansas.

Heath Shuler played football for the Washington Redskins, New Orleans Saints and Oakland Raiders in the NFL from 1994-1998. He served in the U.S. House of Representatives from 2007-2013, representing North Carolina.

Lynn Swann played football for the Pittsburgh Steelers in the NFL from 1974-1982. He ran for Governor of Pennsylvania in 2006 but was not elected. He served on the President's Council on Physical Fitness and Sports from 2002-05.

J.C. Watts played professional football for the Ottawa Rough Riders and the Toronto Argonauts in the Canadian Football League. He served in the U.S. House of Representatives from 1995-2003, representing Oklahoma.

Bob Hope led USO tours to entertain military troops over five decades.
Hope is pictured being given the Medal of Merit
for his service by General Dwight D. Eisenhower.

Chapter 11

PUBLIC SERVICE ANNOUNCEMENTS

N on-profit organizations and the causes they promote are greatly served by enlightening the public. Public education is an important part of the charge for those organizations.

The earliest PSAs promoted the selling of war bonds and were shown in movie theatres during World War I and II. The campaigns included: "Loose lips sink ships" and "Keep 'em rolling." With the advent of radio in the 1920s and its popularity in the 1930s and 1940s, it was a natural sign-off for national shows to include public service messages. Local stations began airing PSAs during their programming to fill the holes when they had not sold all the commercial availabilities. Then, there were Community Calendar shows. Every disc jockey had their favorite causes, and talk shows often featured representatives of non-profit organizations to discuss their services.

When television hit in the late 1940s, public service advertising was institutionalized. PSAs were aired, just as had been done on radio. Local TV stations promoted non-profit organizations via recorded and live spots, ID slides and crawls of calendar items in local communities.

Some of the famous campaigns included annual United Way appeals, Smokey the Bear ("Only you can prevent forest fires"), McGruff, the dog ("Take a bite out of crime"), the United Negro College Fund ("A mind is a terrible thing to lose"), Just Say No to Drugs, the American Cancer Society ("Fight cancer with a check-up and a check"), anti-smoking campaigns, voter awareness, vaccinations, immunizations, educational programs, etc.

Many famous public service campaigns were created by The Advertising Council. This was a consortium of advertising agencies who lent their creativity on a volunteer basis to a variety of causes. These ads won awards for creativity and spurred participating agencies to serve their clients and communities by their volunteer service. Other PSAs were devised by public relations agencies and the non-profit organizations themselves.

The Partnership for a Drug-Free America was founded in New York City in 1985. It was a consortium of advertising agencies who produced public service messages discouraging drug use. It coordinated campaigns with the federal government in its efforts to stem the spread of illegal drugs.

Entertainment shows got into the public service mode. Popular cop show "Highway Patrol" featured its star Broderick Crawford, at the end of each crime-fighting episode, delivering messages on public safety: "Reckless driving doesn't determine who's right, only who's left. If you care to drive, drive with care. It isn't the car that kills; it's the driver. Try to be as good a driver as you think you are. Leave your blood at the Red Cross or at your community blood bank, not on the highway. No matter how new, the safest device in your car is you. The laws of your community are enforced for your protection; obey them. The careless driver isn't driving his car; he's aiming it. It isn't what you drive, but how you drive that counts. The clowns at the circus, they're real funny, but on the highway, they're murder. We'll see you next week." That was the TV show that invented the sign-off "Ten Four," which was subsequently adopted by real police departments.

Another popular TV star of the 1950s and early 1960s was Ronald Reagan, host of "General Electric Theatre." He delivered public spirited messages, which propelled his public persona enough to be elected Governor of California and President of the United States.

National PSAs tend to be image awareness for high-profile causes. Some highlight campaigns and fund-raising appeals. Local PSAs tend to be more specific, including:

- Image
- Campaign
- Cause awareness.
- Phone number to call.
- Special events.
- Cause to support.
- Fund raising.
- Collaboration with other groups.
- Prevention of disease.
- Support of the arts.
- Educational initiatives.
- Spread the word about social concerns.
- Inform and motivate the public.
- Volunteer recruitment.
- Appeals for help.
- Announcements of services, locations, times and delivery criteria.
- Take the cause to the next level.
- Cause related marketing by companies.
- Illuminate on humanitarianism and how citizens can get involved.

PSAs have had a massive impact on our culture. They steered many people into lives committed to community stewardship and leadership.

I have had a fondness and respect for public service announcements for many years. I began my career at age 10 at a radio station. I was a DJ and started writing PSAs, interfacing with people from the non-profit organizations.

In the old days, broadcasting was regulated. Stations had to reapply for their licenses from the Federal Communications Commission every three years. We were required to keep Public Files of correspondence from the listeners and community stakeholders. We were required to perform Community

Ascertainment, a process by which we interviewed leaders on problems of the municipality and how our station might help to address them. Through all that, I became enamored with community service, developing trust relationships with stakeholders.

As the years progressed, I was asked to design public service campaigns, locally and nationally. Often, my work extended beyond the PSAs and to strategic planning the programs themselves. These included some memorable experiences:

For the Houston Police Department were three campaigns: "The Badge Means You Care," "Reach For It" (seatbelt safety) and the Neighborhood Oriented Policing program.

For UNICEF, I worked with celebrity spokespersons Audrey Hepburn and Vincent Price. I got to direct both stars.

For Neighborhood Centers, I wrote and produced the longest running TV PSA, for CHATTERS, a latchkey children's program, running a total of 12 years.

I put together a food bank and literacy organizations, resulting in the campaign "Food for Thought," then got a corporate sponsor (Chevron) to support it.

For United Way, I wrote two campaign themes: "The You in United Way" and "You're Doing So Much for So Many."

One night, I was dining at a restaurant and witnessed children acting out behavior at one table, while being noticed askance by other diners. That inspired me to write a series of PSAs. I got the idea from watching the soap opera "As the World Turns," where tables at a restaurant play out dysfunctional behavior, with other tables watching in review. Each of the five spots focused on one table, played out the dialog and ended with the tagline: "Even the best of families have the worst of times. With appropriate help, you can get through it. Houston Child Guidance Center, a United Way agency, phone number." We shot those mini-dramas in the style of soap operas. Thus, the TV stations ran our PSAs during daytime programming, in lieu of network promos.

The best compliment that I received was from the TV station public service directors: "We run everything that you send us. You know our needs and audiences." Once, I asked the directors if they had special time-slot needs beyond the traditional 30-second spots. They replied that they needed 10-second and 20-second spots. To meet that request, I produced a series of 16 different spots for the YWCA, shot in music video style, focusing on each program service area. The tagline was "YWCA: Always Here, Then + Now." I was inspired to use the plus graphic from the name of a certified public accounting firm, Deloitte Haskins + Sells (which happened to be my client at the time). We premiered those PSAs at a YWCA banquet, followed by a documentary on the agency. That campaign earned seven awards.

There were others. For Gulf Coast Legal Foundation, we dramatized issues related to poverty, with the tagline: "Nobody set out to be poor, and it's not fair. A compassionate and just legal system can help." Restaurateur Ninfa Laurenzo appearing as an advocate at a battered children's shelter. Athletes and entertainers celebrating the anniversary of NASA's landing on the moon, followed by a series for the Challenger Center.

For Midtown Art Center, we projected the "Fabric of the Community." For the Texas General Land Office, we generated the "Buy Recycled" campaign. For the Association for Organ Procurement Organizations, the program built alliances in many communities. For the Texas Department of Human Services, the ESP program encouraged citizens to get off welfare and train for the job market. The Asian American Heritage Foundation fostered multi-cultural programs.

That work resulted in me serving on boards of non-profits and getting recognition for the pro-bono work (culminating in a Lifetime Achievement Award in 2015). That spawned my overall commitment to the work of non-profit organizations, exemplified by this book.

Newspapers began contributing space to non-profit causes back in the 1930s, plus writing stories on many of the programs. Community newspapers followed suit in the 1950s, 1960s and 1970s.

The billboard industry began offering free public service facings to non-profit organizations in the 1960s. As public opposition to billboards as environmental blockages increased, its industry made efforts to work with non-profit organizations to get their words out. In the 1990s, I testified to my city council on behalf of the billboard industry. I stated that they would never get rid of the signs, and their best strategy would be to work with the industry, assuring that local non-profits would be served through PSA boards.

Then came my next time to testify, and recalling this incident makes me sad. I testified before the U.S. Congress, begging them NOT to deregulate broadcasting. I was there in support of non-profit organizations and said that deregulation would be a death-knell to public service advertising on radio and TV. I said that unless the FCC requires PSA quotas to broadcasters, they would not deliver the time. I opined that a handful of mega-corporations would ultimately own broadcasting frequencies and would not have the same public service commitment as did the "mom and pop" broadcasters that they purchased. Sadly, history has proven me to be correct.

Because of deregulation, non-profit organizations were forced to buy time on radio and TV. Many got corporate sponsors to pay the freight. Others cut into programs and services in order to fund marketing. That is exhibited when you see every competing educational institution buying airtime to promote their services to the community. I performed a management study for my state comptroller's office. I reviewed the costs of public awareness campaigns on behalf of state agencies. I opined that agencies felt compelled to spend funds to compete with each other in the arena of marketing.

New forms of public service announcements have emerged to take the place of lost free time on radio and TV. In the 1980s, I started producing filler ads for community newspapers. They were laid out in the style of paid advertising and were furnished as camera-ready copy for newspapers, in the most-needed space fillers as the newspapers had. Thus, they were used.

In the 21st Century, I believe that the future for public service announcements lies on-line. Every non-profit has its own website, and most have blogs in order to disseminate public awareness messages. Many non-profit organizations are producing videos for YouTube.

Now for something new, yet I've been advocating this since 1997. I believe that corporate websites are the most untapped source for public service messages. I encourage corporations to have a Community Corner on their homepages. Highlight the causes that they support. Put filler ads for non-profit groups on their websites. Encourage their customers and stakeholders to support their designated causes. Non-profit organizations need the support of Cause Related Marketing.

Here are some final tips for non-profit organizations in constructing their public service campaigns:

- Carefully choose your topic. Create plausible narratives.
- Research the marketplace and your cause for support.
- Consider your audience. Get reactions from your audiences.
- Get the attention of stakeholders carefully and tastefully.

Hank Moore with Audrey Hepburn, photo taken in 1990, working together on public awareness for UNICEF. Miss Hepburn traveled the world to address issues of hunger, poverty and access to healthcare.

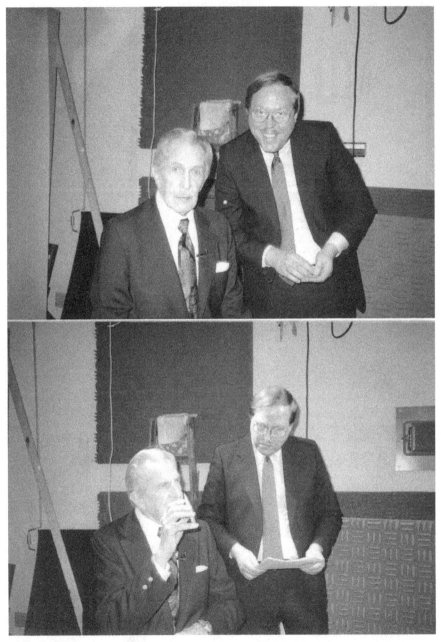

Hank Moore with Vincent Price, photo taken in 1987, producing TV public service spots for UNICEF. This campaign covered growth monitoring, oral rehydration, breast feeding of infants and child immunizations.

We love.

We learn.

We teach.

We are foster parents.

Harris County Children's Protective Services

Foster Parent Program

(713) 626-5701

Somos familia . . .
con amor para dar.

**SOMOS UNA
FAMILIA
TEMPORAL**

Harris County Children's
Protective Services

Foster Parent Program

(713) 626-5701

Keep Texas Beautiful, Inc.

**1993 Texas Environmental
Expo and Festival**

October 15 -16

George R. Brown Convention Center
Houston, Texas

Join Texans working together
for a clean and beautiful Texas.

- Families   - Individuals
- Business   - Government

For more information call
1-800-CLEAN-TX

Admission free to children under 18.

Amour Amour
Heart Ball 1986

Starring
TONY BENNETT
DINING/DANCING/AUCTIONS
Benefiting The American Heart Association
FEBRUARY 14, 1986
CALL 797-1812 FOR TICKETS
AND AUCTION DONATIONS

**American Heart
Association**
Texas Affiliate

What does a full shopping bag
have to do with recycling?

EVERYTHING!

It takes three steps
for recycling to work

- collecting and sorting

- use of recyclables to
  make new products

- using recycled goods

Unless you're *re-using* recycled materials
by buying recycled products, you are not
closing the recycling loop.

Don't let a good thing go to waste.

BuyRecycled

Texas General Land Office

Continue the Legacy . . .
Join the
Community Literacy
Corps:

- Tutors
- Program Volunteers
- Administrative Volunteers
- Business Resources

The
Houston
READ
Commission

Leading the Way to Literacy

(713) 228-1800

*Author Hank Moore wrote these ads for non-profit organizations, which
ran free of charge in newspapers and magazines. Media are happy to run
camera-ready public service messages, on a space-available basis.*

How Advertising that costs you nothing helps solve problems that cost you plenty

The surest way to make a problem worse is to pretend it isn't there.

The safest way to handle a problem is to de-fuse it before it explodes.

The Advertising Council believes that the strength of American democracy is its willingness to use the *voluntary* way to solve problems, before resorting to compulsion. The contribution of the Council is to enlist the talent of the advertising industry so that 195 million Americans may have a better understanding of the problems before them.

On these pages are the familiar symbols of the 18 advertising campaigns now being handled by The Advertising Council, and advertisements from just two of the campaigns: Job Retraining and Racial Relations.

There are no easy answers to these questions. But there can be no solutions at all until there is informed public consciousness.

Then, solutions are possible. This has been proved by the billions of dollars raised by The Advertising Council's past work for United Community Campaigns, the Red Cross, U.S. Savings Bonds and the Colleges. It is proved

by the 425,000 square miles of forest land that Smokey the Bear has saved you to date, by the success of Peace Corps recruiting, and by many other examples.

Today, the resources of advertising can tackle almost any job.

And this 265 million dollars worth of advertising costs you nothing! All of the public service of The Advertising Council is made possible by contributions from American business.

Advertising agency men and women donate time and effort to create the Council's advertising messages. Magazines like this one, newspapers, radio and television stations, networks, and their advertisers, transit advertising and outdoor poster companies donate time and space to keep those messages in your mind.

This is uncommon advertising for the common good.

The Advertising Council
... for public service

If you would like to know more about this work, write for a free booklet to: The Advertising Council, 25 West 45th Street, New York, New York 10036

Retraining (Automation)

Youth Fitness

Aid to Colleges

Balance of Payments

Forest Fires Prevention

Keep America Beautiful

Peace Corps Volunteers

United Community Campaigns

Religion in American Life

American Red Cross

United Nations

Equal Employment Opportunity

Traffic Safety

United Service Organizations

U.S. Savings Bonds

Better Racial Relations

Radio Free Europe Fund

Mental Retardation

This was a trade ad publication from 1960, where the Advertising Council discussed its public service support of worthwhile causes.

ELDERLY

SERVICES

NEIGHBORHOOD CENTERS

Today's Army wants to join you.

WE'VE GOT OVER 300 GOOD, STEADY JOBS.

Se

Se, selenium, shown here in crystallized form, appears to play a vital role in maintaining the integrity of voluntary muscle. In minute amounts, it has proved curative in certain animal dystrophies. Yet its toxicity is so great that it cannot be administered to human patients until its properties and metabolism have been thoroughly investigated.

You can support such fundamental research by your contribution to

**MUSCULAR DYSTROPHY
ASSOCIATIONS OF AMERICA, INC.**
1790 Broadway, New York, N.Y. 10019

*These are examples of public service literature for Neighborhood Centers, the
American Diabetes Association, Muscular Dystrophy and the U.S. Army.*

Chapter 12

STRATEGIC PLANNING FOR NON-PROFIT ORGANIZATIONS

E very business, professional association or non-profit organization goes through cycles in its life. To assume that definitive cycles do not occur is to bury one's head in the sand. To predict and predate the cycles means greater success…earlier than fate would have it.

At any point, each program is in a different phase from others. The astute organization assesses the status of each program and orients its team members to meet constant change and fluctuation.

Phases in the life cycle of every organization include:

1. Conception. A great idea is born, and everyone is off and running.
2. Birth. The decision is made to form a company.
3. Childhood. The organization starts to swell, and its people learn the ropes.
4. Youth. Through trial and error, a slow, steady growth occurs.
5. Maturity. The organization reaches its stride.

6. Stagnation. The bureaucratic mindset takes over. Running an entity is more important than remaining consistent to the company vision (which may have never existed or been developed).
7. Decline. Losses abound: people, processes, market share and enthusiasm. This is a signal to take actions to rejuvenate the enthusiasm and, hopefully, to launch a new growth curve in the company's next era.
8. Death. There is no use for the organization. It has played out.

Position #8 is not an option, and Strategic Planning should not wait until #7 (decline) before embarking upon the process. The best time to regularly implement Strategic Planning programs are at every stage, #1-5. Thus, stagnation will rarely ever occur, and the organization cannot go into a decline.

Strategic planning fulfills a variety of practical and useful purposes. It constitutes disciplined thinking about the organization, its environment and its future. It facilitates the identification of conflicts in perspective. It provides the reinforcement of team building and cohesion. It is a vehicle for monitoring organizational progress.

Strategic Planning is a road map for company growth and progress. Each strategic plan should include these elements:

• Mission statement—Why we are in operation.
• Vision—What we want to become. It fulfills the mission.
• Goals—Broad statements of direction.
• Objectives—What we wish to accomplish.
• Tactics—Specific action steps to reach goals.

In order to be an effective strategic plan, it must be effective, measurable, motivating, realistic, holistic and consistent with the culture of the organization. Since most organizations do not have corporate cultures, the strategic planning process tends to evolve one.

Every strategic plan should draw upon the organization's history. Depending upon the nature of the company, it should be 2-5 years in duration, with revisions annually. Realistic plans must contain attainable goals that can be measured for success. Writing of the plan should involve as many people in the organization as possible.

Many events and circumstances draw an organization to realize that a comprehensive look at its future is essential. At this crossroads, eight strategic questions must be asked of the organization:

1. Do you have financial projections for the next year in writing?
2. Do you have goals for the next year in writing?
3. Are the long-range strategic planning and budgeting processes integrated?
4. Are planning activities consolidated into a written organizational plan?
5. Do you have a written analysis of organizational strengths and weaknesses?
6. Do detailed action plans support each major strategy?
7. Do you have a detailed, written analysis of your market area?
8. Is there a Big Picture?

Strategic planning is not something that happens once and for all. Leadership should examine their organization's strategy and initiate and periodically re-initiate the strategic planning process when any of the following conditions exist:

1. There seems to be a need to change the direction of the organization.
2. There is a need to step up growth and improve profitability.
3. There is a need to develop better information to help management make better decisions.
4. Management is concerned that resources are not concentrated on important things.
5. Management expresses a need for better internal coordination of company activities.
6. The environment in which the organization competes is rapidly changing.
7. There is a sense that company operations are out of control.
8. Management of the organization seems tired or complacent.
9. Management is cautious and uncertain about the company's future.

Differentiation should now be made of the different kinds of planning processes that businesses utilize. Many refer to one when they are thinking of or actually needing another. Though none of these can substitute for a Strategic Plan, each is a component of the larger, more holistic future projection process:

A business plan is a front-end document, enough to get initial financing. An operational plan addresses facilities, policies and procedures. Sales and marketing plans address business development.

If one believes vendors and niche consultants, the definition of Growth Strategies are what their specialty is. It may be: human resources organization, training, technology, health and wellness, sales, marketing, advertising, public relations, core business and life coaching. Few of those have actually written Strategic Plans and do not really comprehend what the Visioning process actually is.

Steps in the Strategic Planning Process

Although every strategic planning process is uniquely designed to fit the specific needs of a particular organization, every successful model includes most of these steps.

Vision. Identification of the organization's vision and mission is the first step of any strategic planning process. The vision sets out the reasons for organization's existence and the "ideal" state that it aims to achieve.

Mission. The mission identifies major goals and performance objectives. Both are defined within the framework of the organizations philosophy and are used as a context for development and evaluation of intended and emergent strategies. One cannot overemphasize the importance of a clear vision and mission. None of the subsequent steps will matter if the organization is not certain where it is headed.

Environmental Scan. Once the vision and mission are clearly identified, the organization must analyze its external and internal environment. The environmental scan analyzes information about organization's external environment (economic, social, demographic, political, legal, technological, and international factors), the industry and internal organizational factors.

SWOT Analysis. This is a comprehensive look at the organization's own strengths, weaknesses, opportunities and threats.

Gap Analysis. Organizations evaluate the difference between their current position and desired future through gap analysis. As a result, an organization can develop specific strategies and allocate resources to close the gap and achieve its desired state.

Benchmarking. Measuring and comparing the organization's operations, practices and performance against others is useful for identifying "best" practices. Through an ongoing systematic benchmarking process, organizations find a reference point for setting their own goals and targets. The 10 most common benchmarking mistakes are: (1) Internal processes are unexamined. (2) Site visits "feel good" but do not elicit substantive data or ideas. (3) Questions and goals are vague. (4) The effort is too broad or has too many parameters. (5) The focus is general and not upon actual processes. (6) The team is not fully committed to the effort. (7) Homework and/or advanced research is not assigned and conducted. (8) The wrong subjects for benchmarking are selected. (9) The effort fails to look outside its own organization and industry. (10) No follow-up action is taken.

Strategic Issues. The organization determines its strategic issues based on (and consistent with) its vision and mission, within the framework of environmental and other analyses. Strategic issues are the fundamental issues the organization has to address to achieve its mission and move towards its desired future.

Strategic Programming. To address strategic issues and develop deliberate strategies for achieving their mission, organizations set strategic goals, action plans and tactics during the strategic programming stage. Strategic goals are the milestones the organization aims to achieve which evolve from the strategic issues. The SMART goals model is essential to setting meaningful goals. Smart goals are specific, measurable, agreed upon, realistic and time/cost bound. Action plans define how the organization gets to where it needs to go and the steps required to reach strategic goals. Tactics are specific actions used to achieve the strategic goals and implement the strategic plans.

Emergent Strategies. Unpredicted and unintended events frequently occur that differ from the organization's intended strategies, and the organization must respond. Emergent strategy is a pattern, a consistency of behavior over time, a realized pattern that was not expressly intended in the original planning of strategy. It results from a series of actions converging into a consistent pattern.

Evaluation of Strategy. Periodic evaluations of strategies, tactics and action programs are essential to assessing success of the strategic planning process. It is important to measure performance at least annually (but preferably more often), to evaluate the effect of specific actions on long-term results and on the organization's vision and mission. The organization should measure current performance against previously set expectations and consider any changes or events that may have impacted the desired course of actions.

Review of the Strategic Plan. After assessing the progress of the strategic planning process, the organization needs to review the strategic plan, make necessary changes and adjust its course based on these evaluations. The revised plan must take into consideration emergent strategies and changes affecting the organization's intended course.

Thinking More Strategically. With time, people in the organization routinely make their decisions within the framework of the organization's strategic vision and plan. Strategic planning becomes an organizational norm, deeply embedded within the organization's decision-making process, and participants learn to think strategically as part of their regular daily activities Strategic thinking involves analyzing options against a range of alternatives and decisions that will chart the organization's future course.

Content Outline, Major Headings for a Strategic Plan

1. Program-Service Development (Core Business)
   Establish points of difference, overcome misperceptions and own niche segments.
   Development and sophistication of current programs-services.
   Roles, responsibilities and functions for each contributor to programs.
   Recognizing and demanding quality in work output.
   Diversification of programs-services.
2. Running the Organization
   Divisionalization

Time management, just-in-time delivery and other business-accepted efficiencies.

Re-engineering to accomplish the greatest possible efficiencies, results and objectives.

3. Financial

Portfolio planning.

Fiduciary responsibility.

Fund raising activities.

Relationships with funding sources.

Exploring new streams of revenue.

Financial and technological resources.

Accountability to all stakeholders.

4. Professional Resources, Human Capital

Diversity is the fundamental thread that makes the organization necessary and successful.

Human Resources, staffing the programs.

Training for service providers, associates and employees

Team building.

Ongoing professional development and mentoring each other.

Cross-applying talents and experiences from one program to the other.

5. Business Development, Community Outreach

Selling and marketing the organization to desired constituencies.

Development of community contacts and resources.

6. The Organization's Long-term Goals

Taking focus.

Corporate culture adjustment, evolving into corporate mindset.

Collaborations, joint-venturing and partnering.

Develop and maintain benchmarks for quality assurance and compliance by all resources.

7. Planning for the Future

Ultimate evolution into new strata of service delivery.

Strategic planning for the entire organization.

Utilize, learn from and benefit from previous planning efforts.

Linkage of benefits from planned, orderly growth.

Hold Think Tanks and retreats.

Keep focus of all above operations in relation to where the organization is headed long-term.

Reasons to Support Planning

Human beings live to attract goals. Organizations get people caught in activity traps…unless managers periodically pull back and reassess in terms of goals. Managers lose sight of their employees' goals. Employees work hard, rather than productively. Mutually agreed-upon goals are vital.

People caught in activity traps shrink, rather than grow, as human beings. Hard work that produces failures yields apathy, inertia and loss of self-esteem. People become demeaned or diminished as human beings when their work proves meaningless. Realistic goals can curb this from happening.

Failure can stem from either non-achievement of goals or never knowing what they were. The tragedy is both economic and humanistic. Unclear objectives produce more failures than incompetence, bad work, bad luck or misdirected work.

When people know and have helped set their goals, their performance improves. The best motivator is knowing what is expected and analyzing one's one performance relative to mutually agreed-upon criteria.

Goal attainment leads to ethical behavior. The more that an organization is worth, the more worthy it becomes. Most management subsystems succeed or fail according to the clarity of goals of the overall organization.

To ascertain goals, we can examine problems, study the organization's core business, look at Strengths, Weaknesses, Opportunities and Threats. To make goal setting a reality, start at the top to adopt a policy of strategic planning. Strategic goals and objectives must filter downward throughout all the organization. Training is vital. Continual follow-up, refinement and new goal setting must ensue. Programs must be competent, effective and benchmarked. A corporate culture must foster all goal setting, policies, practices and procedures.

Use indicators and indices wherever they can be used. Use common indicators where categories are similar, and use special indicators for special jobs. Let your people participate in devising the indicators. Make all indicators meaningful, and retest them periodically. Use past results as only one indicator for the future. Have a reason for setting all indicators in place. Indicators are not ends in themselves, only a means of getting where the organization needs to go. Indicators must promote action. Discard those that stifle action.

Utilize outside consultants. Do not conduct all planning internally. Keep objectivity.

Budget enough time. Keep the procedure simple and disciplined. Develop the plan in stages. Set specific objectives. Set policies from this document. Ensure that the plan meets organizational needs.

Find and keep a champion. Involve those who will implement the plan. Don't spread resources too thinly. Communicate results of the process to affected parties.

Tailor actions to the organization's culture. Be willing to change as the process matures. Be open minded. Apply feedback to the continuing planning process. Keep the plan alive.

These are the benefits of Strategic Planning: Enhance problem prevention capabilities of the organization. Group based strategic decisions reflect the best available alternatives. Team motivation should be enhanced. Gaps and overlaps in activities should reduce. Resistance to change should be reduced.

Chapter 13

OUTLINE FOR NON-PROFIT STRATEGIC PLAN

Sample from a plan for a social service organization

Mission Statement—Why we are in operation.

Vision—What we want to become. It fulfills the mission.

Goals—Broad statements of direction.

Objectives—What we wish to accomplish.

Tactics—Specific action steps to reach goals.

Mission Statement—Why we are in operation.

The agency will foster and administer high quality programs, training and support services for the benefit of children and families in all strata of the area, focusing its efforts toward identifying and filling niches for information and referral, direct services and community stewardship.

Vision—What we want to become.

- Be a community initiator, organizer and leader in social service, family, youth and human empowerment issues and programs.

- Prepare the community for pro-active changes in society through well planned, executed and monitored programs and services.
- Be an active, dynamic change agent, flexible in operations to identify, understand, meet and exceed community needs.
- Remain a source and inspiration for partnering among service providers. Educate constituencies on the importance and economic benefits of collaborations.
- Conduct business in fiscally and ethically responsible manners. Be accountable and responsive to our clients, colleagues, funding sources, employees, volunteers, corporate supporters, the community, public sector regulators and other constituencies.

Core Organizational Values

A. Internal

- Enjoy serving children and families.
- Employees are empowered, highly invested in the success of the agency.
- Like to find innovative approaches to problems.
- Must maintain financial equilibrium, in order to continue doing fine work.
- Intend to remain business-like and economically responsible.

B. External

- Supports framework, welfare and nurturing of the family structure.
- Children and youth are our future.
- By adults reflecting back upon the childhood experience, they become enriched and become part of the family visioning process.
- Have always collaborated, out of necessity, and always will do so.
- Collaboration, teamwork and innovatively filling niches is a way of life.

Goals—Broad statements of direction.

- Establish and market fee-for-service programs.
- Develop a sophisticated inter-relationship of agency programs to each other.

- Uncover and strive to address community needs, as they are first evidenced.
- Maintain standards of community accountability.
- Move toward taking on more of a consultant role...program administrator.
- Be an innovator for other family service agencies.
- Research function, developing technical base.
- Stay atop government trends and public policy issues.
- Create more private sector partnerships.
- Create and sustain a "point of difference," in order to gain further support.
- Become "top of the mind" to key constituencies.

Objectives, with Tactics for each Key Results Area:

- Objectives—What we wish to accomplish.
- Tactics—Specific action steps to reach goals.

Financial—Administrative

Objective 1: Update and streamline the controller office and contract administration processes.

> Tactic 1: Select and train new business manager.
>
> Tactic 2: Financial services policies are reviewed by staff, board and accounting consultant, with recommendations for streamlining made.
>
> Tactic 3: Business services plan for next five years (an addendum to the Strategic Plan) is compiled and presented to the board.

Objective 2: Acquire a M.I.S. system that will serve agency needs for the next 3+ years.

> Tactic 1: New business manager studies office systems and makes own internal recommendations by date.
>
> Tactic 2: Work with consulting firms to identify and price computer systems, presenting recommendations to the board by date.
>
> Tactic 3: Board determines financial viabilities of investing in M.I.S. equipment and establishes timeline for acquisition, by date.

Financial—Fund Raising

Objective 1: Create stable funding sources.

Tactic 1: Listing of the agency's leading funding sources.

Tactic 2: Board appoints Fund Raising Committee.

Tactic 3: Committee studies current funding structure and levels, making recommendations for future strategies.

Tactic 4: Fund Raising Committee writes a plan for next five years (addendum to the Strategic Plan), compiled and presented to the board.

Objective 2: Maintain marketplace sensitivity toward changing funding sources.

Tactic 1: Board designates a staff member, with responsibility for Development.

Tactic 2: Participating in funding and grant activities becomes a part of every board and staff member's job description.

Objective 3: Enhanced stature with the United Way, with increased profile and higher funding (allocations and project grants).

Tactic 1: Get input from the United Way in devising the Fund Raising Plan.

Tactic 2: Seek appropriations increases for at least 5% over each previous year.

Tactic 3: Seek at least one special project grant from United Way each year, devising programs to meet emerging and stated needs.

Tactic 4: Pursue a relationship building program with United Way.

Objective 4: Contracts from other providers and non-profit organizations.

Objective 5: Conduct an annual special event: the Family Expo.

Objective 6: Fees from services, training and other programs.

Tactic 1: Current fee structure is reviewed by staff in report form, with recommendations for modifications, completed.

Tactic 2: Sliding scale fee program to get paying clients into child care centers is developed by staff.

Tactic 3: Consultation, training and management of corporate child care programs is developed by staff.

Objective 7: Collateral materials, licensing agreements.

Tactic 1: Fund Raising Committee and staff strategize the viability of preparing and marketing workbooks and other training materials.

Quality

Objective 1: Set, meet and exceed standards by which the agency is regulated.

Tactic 1: Quality Management Committee for the overall agency to be appointed by the Executive Director. Includes a representative of each major program component, board and Advisory Council.

Tactic 2: Committee to meet monthly, developing a quality management plan, an addendum to this Strategic Plan.

Tactic 3: Committee to engage United Way (which has quality management resources available), to assist committee in drafting this plan.

Tactic 4: Standards to be observed and included in the quality plan include city, county, state (which are becoming the benchmark criteria), federal.

Tactic 5: Subjects to be observed and included in the quality plan include: Safety, Health, Quality of services, Age appropriateness.

Tactic 6: Quality tenets are to be integrated into subsequent departmental annual plans, attesting to the Council's commitment toward Continuous Quality Improvement.

Objective 2: Seek and obtain additional certifications.

Objective 3: For the overall agency, to be part of the Strategic Plan.

Tactic 1: Each department reviews and continually updates its own objectives.

Tactic 2: This process reflects careful thinking and the caliber of leadership that will catapult the agency in the 21st Century. Convey standards of caring and quality into the work product and atmosphere of professionalism.

Tactic 3: Involve our constituencies (clients, providers, funding sources, collaborators) in the Continuous Quality Improvement process.

Service

Objective 1: Near-capacity occupancy in centers.

Tactic 1: Staff prepares fee for service report, include dynamics on prospective clients' ability to pay, including study competing agencies' occupancy rates, with analysis for their success rates, by date.

Tactic 2: Each center consults parent advisory committees on opportunities to recruit more enrollees and invites parents to attend the open house.

Tactic 3: Studies of competing agencies and other marketplace demographics should reveal other constituencies to tap.

Objective 2: Expand programs into areas of family and social services.

Tactic 1: Staff to investigate and recommend viabilities of pre-school programs with school districts.

Tactic 2: Staff to investigate and recommend viabilities of after-school programs with school districts.

Tactic 3: Staff to investigate and recommend viabilities of homeless care programs with area shelters.

Objective 3: Provide child care to low and moderate income families.

Tactic 1: Limits of the sliding scale are explored in the fee-for-service study.

Tactic 2: Center parent advisory councils shall study further need areas.

Tactic 3: If clients must be transported from other neighborhoods, logistics shall be strategized. This will entail writing a grant for transportation.

Tactic 4: Program is monitored and updated annually.

Objective 4: Training.

Tactic 1: Review of existing and past programs, recommendations for new programs, along with benchmark monitoring

Objective 5: Contract administration.

Tactic 1: Staff determines that system for monitoring contracts parallels the streamlining of the business office.

Tactic 2: Staff to make recommendations to improve efficiency of contracts, by 20% each year, reflected in time savings and economies of scale.

Tactic 3: Staff to write annual plan for departmental operation.

Program Development

Objective 1: Seek and obtain public sector child care contract.

Tactic 1: Program staff ascertains nature and length of existing contracts for such institutions as the Federal government, state agencies, city, county, universities and area school districts.

Tactic 2: As part of program development and fund raising efforts, department heads will interface regularly with public sector contacts.

This networking effort shall be targeted specifically at obtaining more long-term public sector contracts.

Tactic 3: Ascertain which public sector contracts with competing agencies will expire during the year. Add these to the primary target list.

Tactic 4: Reflecting upon the CCMS review, agency must determine areas where it can strengthen capabilities, in order to pursue major administrative contracts. Information of this nature must be shared with the board on a quarterly basis, in order for the agency to develop necessary resources.

Objective 2: Study reactivating the Information and Referral program.

Tactic 1: Executive Director appoints an Information & Referral Committee.

Tactic 2: I&R Committee meets with United Way, studies existing I&R programs in other service areas and makes recommendations on interfacing the I&R program with others in the community.

Objective 3: Start pilot corporate child care program.

Tactic 1: Staff compiles list of corporate child care endorsers.

Tactic 2: Staff holds a focus group with representatives of this list, to discuss viabilities of serving the corporate marketplace.

Tactic 3: Staff develops list of corporate prospects ripe for child care programs, reflecting focus group and other research.

Tactic 4: Staff develops a formal plan for targeting, offering, contacting and marketing child care services to corporate constituencies of all sizes.

Tactic 5: Begin providing services to corporate constituencies.

Staff Development

Objective 1: Job descriptions (Position Results Oriented Description) for every staff member.

Tactic 1: Sample PRODs are given to each department. PROD is a process by which each employee writes their own job description (with supervisor overseeing). Each employee sets his/her benchmarks for success, based upon duties, responsibilities and career path orientation.

Tactic 2: A meeting of all departments is held to discuss their implementation.

Tactic 3: PRODs for each staff member are to be written, edited and implemented.

Tactics 4: Annual staff reviews by the Executive Director shall follow agreed-upon categories in each employee's PROD.

Objective 2: More executive staff.

Tactic 1: Board designates or adds a staff member, with primary responsibility for Development (fund raising).

Tactic 2: Board and Executive Director determine a formal staff progression plan as part of the PROD process.

Objective 3: Professional development.

Tactic 1: This will be a section in each PROD. Each staff member will determine quotas and areas of training, reading and other professional development which he/she will pursue each year.

Tactic 2: Since the agency has acknowledged expertise in training, the agency understands the full value of professional development. Board must give staff the resources to pursue ample professional development activities.

Tactic 3: Council employees will empower each other, including colleagues in traditional and non-traditional training. This will take the primary form of an annual staff retreat, covering executive leadership, community stewardship and agency positioning-development issues, in addition to social service issues and techniques training.

Tactic 4: Employees will determine other collaborative professional development that they can create and undertake in between annual retreats.

Board Development

Objective 1: Add more board members, with specific expertise and interests.

Tactic 1: According to the by-laws, the Board of Directors may have up to 24 members. Be at maximum size of Board.

Tactic 2: A roster of board members is attached in the Appendix of Strategic Plan.

Objective 2: Reflect community representation.

Tactic 1: Board should include full ethnic representation.

Tactic 2: At least two board members should reflect the users of services.

Tactic 3: At least one board member should have fulfilled a lead staff/board role with another major non-profit agency.

Tactic 4: Corporate representation should be diverse and reflect those companies' financial and resource commitments toward the Council (including giving board members ample office time to tend to Council business).

Objective 3: Job descriptions (Position Results Oriented Description) for every board member.

Tactic 1: Sample job descriptions attached in the Appendix of this document

Objective 4: Board manual, orientation sessions and work assignments.

Tactic 1: Executive Director shall prepare a three-ring binder for each board member. Contents include:

- Agency background and history.
- Roster of board members (as stated above).
- Calendar of events for the coming year.
- Copy of the agency's 501 (c)(3) statement.
- Copy of this Strategic Plan, with Appendix.

Tactic 2: Orientation sessions for board members shall be held semi-annually.

Tactic 3: Upon joining the board, each member will have a memorandum that details time commitments, recommended resource allocations and job responsibilities (culminating in each writing their own PROD).

Objective 5: Training for board.

Tactic 1: An annual retreat shall be held. All board members expected to attend.

Tactic 2: Each board member shall be expected to attend one training session presented by the agency for its client base. This will give board members a better insight into what the agency does, and the regular attendance of board members sends an important message to our clients, providers, collaborators and funding sources.

Tactic 3: Each board member shall be expected to visit and tour one of the centers. Visitations shall hence be once every year.

Objective 6: Mentoring, each board member to liaison with a staff member.

Tactic 1: Board chair assigns staff members to board members. Both will communicate informally with each other on aspects of agency operations. This periodic interface is designed to address issues early and identify opportunities to carry the planning process further than this document.

Objective 7: Board appoints an Advisory Council. This shall be an adjunct to the board. It includes community leaders and other resources who lend their name, influence and occasional resources toward the good of the agency.

Promotional-Marketing

Objective 1: Community relations agency promotional program.

Tactic 1: Separate program is an Addendum to this Strategic Plan and shall be updated annually by staff.

Tactic 2: This program shall be directed by staff, with support by board.

Objective 2: Public service campaign.

Tactic 1: Production and distribution completed as part of this Strategic Planning Process.

Objective 3: Name-corporate identity.

Tactic 1: For the time being, the existing name stands. The Strategic Planning Committee believes that the name is strong and leaves latitude for growth. In the coming year, focus group testing of the name will be recommended, with the likely outcome being an updated logo to accompany the same name. A corporate identity program will likely result.

Tactic 2: As the Council expands and adds new programs, a public awareness effort will be even more important.

Objective 4: Process over next two years to become all we want to be and can be.

Tactic 1: This Strategic Plan signals the dawning of a new quarter century in the agency's growth. An expanded awareness toward corporate identity is recommended for the second and third years into this Strategic Plan. Taking the framework and sophisticating the organization will be the emphasis, as the first-year newness of the Strategic Plan has run its course.

Tactic 2: As the corporate identity builds, the agency will want to consider a merger of another non-profit into the agency.

Objective 5: Provisions for updating and modifying, per emerging trends.

Tactic 1: The Strategic Planning Committee (composed of board and staff members shall reconvene at least twice per year, to review progress.

Tactic 2: Every department (including the board) will keep their own scorecard, as to how timeline deadlines were met. Areas of quality will be measured with fair, objective benchmarks, determined by each department.

Objective 6: Buy-in and support by all.

Tactic 1: Every staff member and board member shall read this Strategic Plan and sign the last page of the document.

Tactic 2: Mention of progress in meeting and addressing the Strategic Plan (if only brief discussion) shall hence be a part of every board meeting and every general staff meeting.

Tactic 3: Quality tenets and philosophies of the agency are to be communicated to clients, providers and other external publics.

Tactic 4: Regular reading and review of this Strategic Plan shall be a commitment of the Council. The organization has evolved because of change in the community. To embrace this process is indicative of the agency's willingness to evolve as a role model to the rest of the community.

We, the undersigned, the Board of Directors and staff hereby sign and acknowledge this Strategic Plan, as an affirmation of our shared vision for the agency.

Each signature carries the date in which the final draft of this plan was reviewed.

Appendix

1. Business Services Plan.
2. M.I.S. three-year Plan and Timeline.
3. Fund Raising Committee Plan.
4. Quality Management Committee Plan.
5. Training Plan.
6. Community Services Plan.

7. Other Departmental Plans.
8. Board of Directors Plan.
9. Agency charter and by-laws (with copy of 501 (c)(3) statement).
10. Organizational Charts (board and staff).
11. Sample PROD Job Descriptions.
12. Sample target list of funding prospects.
13. List of contracts in place and due to begin.
    Trend Analyses
    Promotional-Marketing-Community Relations Program
    Follow-up Reviews and Measurements.

Trend Analyses

1. Environment
   - Society is more stressful and dangerous to children now than ever before.
   - Society is inclined to point fingers of blame, guilt and responsibility on schools, churches, community programs and others—anybody but the family units.
   - Social service providers are and always will be over-worked and under-paid.
2. Market for Clients
   - Most parents have to work.
   - Single parent households dominate our constituencies.
   - Low-income families are not all clustered in the same old neighborhoods.
   - Fee-paying clients exist and must be tapped.
3. Competitive Situation
   - New players are entering the industry each year.
   - Competitive pricing, packaging of services and external factors bring new players the contracts.
   - Purchasers of services cannot discern the wanna-be's from the established providers.
   - Competitors need to learn how to ban together, when necessary.

4. Socio Demographics
   - The population is multi-culturally diverse.
   - Minority population percentages will increase.
   - The information explosion has alerted to society to more problems now than ever before, causing a general discontent, weariness and uneasiness about the future of today's youth.
   - Perception is reality. If citizens fear for safety, health, welfare and economic stability, then these are very real issues.
5. The economy
   - Corporate down-sizing will put more people out of work.
   - Not all of the disenfranchised workforce has the adaptability and skill-set to transition to an entrepreneurial mode.
   - More poverty (short-term and long-term) will emerge.
   - The "working poor" will emerge in size, complexity and composition.
   - The private sector is already stretched and cannot endow social service programs at higher (or even the same) levels.
6. Government, Legislature, Congress, City-County, Regulatory Agencies
   - Regulatory and compliance issues are choking child care providers with bureaucracy.
   - Public sector funding is becoming more limited.
   - Politically influenced programs will cut back funding for social services.
   - Public officials know that child care is a "politically correct issue" and need assistance by the industry in championing it properly. The squeaky wheel gets the grease.
   - Building support for and with public officials is essential.
7. Technology
   - Child care is still a personal service-business, based on humanity and people skills.
   - Technology helps teaching techniques and modes of instruction.
   - Technology helps this agency to better manage bureaucratic red tape.
   - Technology assures greater information flow to key publics.

- Technology assures greater accountability to funding sources.
8. Factors Surrounding Service Delivery
   - We can never have and provide enough training, and it is essential.
   - Funding limitations must be recognized and dealt with.
   - Rather than succumbing to societal fears and pressures, we must become re-dedicated toward the agency's purposes (literally and symbolically).
   - We must learn more about our competitors and fight them fairly.
   - We must creatively partner with old and new entities, for collective gain.
   - Every member of the agency's board and staff must play a defined role.
   - There is too much ground to cover. Sliding backwards is not an option.

Strengths

- High perceived credibility among key publics.
- Good product-service rendered.
- Knowledge of the child care and social services industries.
- Experienced staff.
- Track record of longevity, adaptability and flexibility.

Weaknesses

- Insufficient resources…financial and human.
- No public visibility.
- Lack of home base…identifiable building.
- Need more executive leadership.
- Need more identifiable roles and duties for board members.

Opportunities

- Showcase family issues.
- Name change or modification in corporate identity.
- Be a voice of the social services industry.

- Refine programs to be publicly showcased.
- Garner support and give thanks to supporters.

Threats

- New entrants to the industry are treading our ground, starting programs and getting funding.
- Those whom we have trained are now representing themselves as trainers and full-scope social service resources.
- Funding for social services is tight.
- Corporate resources are stretched.

Timeline for the Strategic Plan

Chapter 14

BOARD DEVELOPMENT

Keepers of the Flame
Briefing for Board of Directors Members

Board members represent the best and brightest in their own organizations. Serving corporations, associations and community organizations is an obligation and trust. If service is best rendered, then all involved will benefit.

Persons who are recruited for and commit to service on boards of directors have several important responsibilities, per categories on my Business Tree™, including:

1. The business you're in. Visit programs and become knowledgeable about the organization's work. Don't spend all your board time in meetings. Get to know senior staff, in your areas of expertise. Become an informed advocate.

2. Running the business. Study the organization's reason for being and how it operates. Be sure that you are committed to its mission and have abilities to expand it. Boards provide counsel to management but should not get involved in the day-to-day affairs of running the organization.

3. Financial. Board members have fiduciary responsibility, authority and liability for all business operations. Learn to read and understand budgets. Understand the internal controls, unrelated business income tax and accountability.

4. People. Your time is your most precious commodity. Spend it wisely, doing homework about the organization that you represent. Factor in support time by your family and business colleagues. When all share in the responsibilities, then all can share in the pride of achievement.

5. Business development. Realize that board participation is, likewise, a commitment of your company. Understand that necessary out-of-pocket expenses and time expenditures of your employees will be borne by you and/or your company. Board service benefits your business, your association and your industry. Strategize that all are impacted optimally.

6. Body of Knowledge. Understand "the competition." Every organization competes with others, in some shape or fashion. Study the competition and marketplace, so that opportunities to exchange ideas, collaborate or meet newly identified community niches may be feasible.

7. The Big Picture. Strategic planning and building a shared vision are prerequisites for every board of directors. To succeed in trying times, every board member must contribute to the organization's future and advocate actions that assure that pro-active change occurs.

Boards must represent the shareholders and all other stakeholders. They have the ultimate authority in guiding the affairs of the corporation. They are responsible for corporate affairs and the selection and supervision of officers. Boards set the policies and work with management in conducting the strategic planning and visioning. Officers are responsible for the procedures and actions. The power and authority lie within the entire board.

Board members are required to act within their authority, exercise due care and observe fiduciary responsibilities. Breach of any of these duties could result in liabilities on the part of the directors and the overall organization.

Challenges for Boards of Directors

Since the corporate scandals, board members have been under a microscope with brighter lights aimed at them. Some corporations have had a difficult time in recruiting the best possible board members. That's in part because they sought the same types of people from limited niches where board members were chosen in the first place.

It is vital for organizations to reach out to new constituencies for their boards. It means recruiting enlightened individuals with vision and the inclination to inspire others toward creative business approaches. Outside directors should reflect all aspects of the business, not just core business and financial.

The ideal board member should:

- Have a bias for action.
- Communicate ideas to diverse constituencies.
- Draw upon business background for making decisions.
- Maintain objectivity at all times.
- Devote time and energies toward board service.
- Have insights into people and problems.
- Be a team player.
- Understand the art of compromise.
- Take action, even on controversial matters.
- Have the ability to inspire.
- Prepare for all board meetings.
- Attend all board meetings.
- Support and promote the organization at every possible occasion.

As part of the corporate reform movement, boards of directors, once recruited and organized, should operate as efficiently and professionally as the business units of the company in question.

There should exist a deliberate board evaluation initiative, with the specific goal of identifying ways to do a better job of governing and protecting the shareholders. Policies and procedures should encompass the Board Self-Evaluation, including checklists and principles on evaluating activities and effectiveness of the board.

Questions to ask in self-evaluation might include: Are we constructively engaged with management in determining corporate strategy and does management think so? Have we shown leadership and vision at creating that strategy? Are we providing the necessary strategic thinking, oversight and advice? Are we effectively monitoring and supporting management's execution of the strategy? Is the board able to respond in a timely way to indications that a change in strategy is needed? How are we structured to be agents of change?

The evaluation can focus on board structure, asking questions such as whether the board has the right skill set, profile and committee structure.

The evaluation can focus on board meetings, asking such questions as whether the materials prepare the board for necessary discussions and whether there is sufficient time for directors to meet independently of management.

The evaluation can focus on board responsibilities, asking questions such as whether board members are satisfied with the CEO performance review process.

Responsibilities of Board Members

Directors may have specific responsibilities that are unique to the business or industry in which they perform service. The directors will also have a variety of responsibilities which are defined in the bylaws of the organization and in numerous federal and state statutes and regulations.

Every board shares a set of general responsibilities that members should be prepared to assume when they serve. The following checklist may be helpful to consider when the board conducts its self-assessment.

1. Organizational Governance. The Board is responsible for setting the strategic directions. The board, in conjunction with the executive staff, defines the directions, programs, services and outreach efforts of the organization.

The Board has responsibility for developing and approving updates to the strategic plan and the associated budget, which defines the programs and initiatives for each fiscal year. Board members have the ultimate fiduciary responsibility and are responsible to assure that the organization is fiscally sound and operated within procedures and policies that are prudent and ethical.

The Board should create and modify the written governing policies of the organization. These include the definition of goals, definition of executive limitations and responsibilities, financial planning, asset protection, code of conduct, Board operations and performance.

The entire Board will review and approve any and all actions of the Executive Committee of the Board, which is empowered to act between Board meetings, and under circumstances when a full Board meeting is not possible.

2. Assurance of Executive Performance. The Board does not conduct the work of the organization, but it must assure that the necessary work is done, through delegation to the Chief Executive Officer.

The performance of the organization is monitored by the Board with internal and external reports and through the ongoing performance appraisals of the CEO. It is important that all Board members recognize that management is the responsibility of the staff. The Board's primary roles are to define policy and to set direction for the organization.

3. Board Governance. The directors create policies and procedures for the governance of the Board. The Board takes the necessary steps to assure that its members are knowledgeable about the organization, including its culture and norms, the profession, the marketplaces it serves, and the roles, responsibilities and performance as a body. The Board nurtures the development of members as a cohesive working group and regularly monitors its performance as a Board.

4. Linkage with the Organization. The Board must develop and maintain healthy relationships with the organization, stay in touch with current issues and set strategic directions. Their role is to act in

the broad best interest of the organization, supporting directions that serve all of its facets.

Directors should not act in a limited or representative role reflective of a given constituency with which they are or have been affiliated. Board members should function as emissaries for their organization.

Recommendations to Directors

Given the need to recruit board members from all professional niches and to delineate their roles and responsibilities. there are specific activities which they could pursue. Here is my suggested briefing to board members, per branch on The Business Tree™:

1. The Business You're In. Know the programs and how they work. Get to know senior staff. Become an informed advocate for the organization and its industry.
2. Running the Business. Employ and supervise the Executive Director. Approve annual plan of work and goals submitted by committees. Adopt rules and procedures for conduct of meetings, as needed. Recommend and approve necessary changes to by-laws or governing documents. Attend board meetings. Serve on committees and task forces to carry out objectives. Attend the annual meeting.
3. Financial. Maintain and champion fiduciary responsibility for all organizational actions. Approve and oversee the annual budget. Approve quarterly and year-end financial statements. Oversee financial transactions.
4. People. Serve as an elected member of a leadership team. Address the needs and problems of the staff in policy decisions. Maintain communication with designated members as Board liaison. Bring aboard new people and new ideas.
5. Business Development, External Relations. Serve as delegate to other organizations. Participate in marketing.
6. Body of Knowledge. Research and understand the competition. Employ lobbyist representatives. Research and understand regulators and other

outside influences. Take part in guiding, monitoring and evaluating organizational performance and effectiveness. Champion change. Accommodate growing pains…as a company evolves from startup to growth toward maturity, the responsibilities and character of its board of directors will evolve as well.

7. The Big Picture. Participate in and champion Strategic Planning and Visioning. Define the mission and participate in strategic planning to review the purposes, priorities, financial standing and goals. Uphold high standards, serving as role models to the organization. Create, interpret and measure policies and strategies. Evaluate how well the board is performing and maintain an effective organization, procedures and recruitment.

In this era following the corporate scandals and anticipating years of corporate reform initiatives, challenges and opportunities for boards and their directors still far outweigh the downsizes. The secret to success is the order in which one prioritizes and maximizes windows of opportunity.

Service on boards is a culmination of a senior business executive's career. It is more than a line on a resume. If conducted correctly, board service will round out the professional and should have spin-off effects for his-her company.

Identification and recruitment of board prospects is an ongoing process. Seek those who have served other organizations well, especially in the non-profit realm. Get referrals from all strata of the community, to assure a diverse board (career orientation, expertise, interests). Determine each board member's true intentions and best capabilities for service.

Offer training for the boards, including an annual retreat (professionally facilitated). Provide a complete manual. Board members should attend staff training and community functions. Education and professional enhancement are the non-profit organization's stock in trade. Keep the communication flow open, sent well in advance of deadlines for action.

Board members who are most successful will budget their time and spend it wisely on behalf of their organizations. Requirements for board meeting attendance and committee participation quotas should be articulated from the outset. The board chair should monitor each board member's activities, to get maximum value for their time, talents and resources.

Board members maintain relationships with the organization, the board itself, the staff, committees and task forces, outside resources and the public. All relationships should be nurtured.

Chapter 15

HISTORY OF PUBLIC MEDIA, NON-PROFIT STATIONS SERVING COMMUNITIES

Public Radio

On January 13, 1910, the first public radio broadcast was an experimental transmission of a live Metropolitan Opera House program, headlined by Enrico Caruso. Commercial radio developed, and there was programming devoted to public service, public affairs and cultural enrichment.

Local stations were licensed by the Federal Communications Commission. They were required to conduct Community Ascertainment as the basis for license renewal. Stations asked community leaders about problems and challenges in the community, with the expectation that news and public affairs programming might address some of those issues. Stations were required to maintain Public Files of correspondence, community engagement and activities that would be deemed as serving the public trust.

In the 1920s, radio stations that were non-commercial began operation. Most were licensed to educational institutions and some to cities. In 1925, the Association of College and University Broadcasting Stations was formed, renamed the National Association of Educational Broadcasters in 1934.

In 1951, NAEB established a Tape Network to distribute programs, shared from local stations. It evolved as the National Educational Radio Network, which began broadcasting on six radio stations on April 3, 1961. As a result of the Public Broadcasting Act of 1967, NERN became part of National Public Radio on February 26, 1970. The Corporation for Public Broadcasting created the Public Broadcasting Service and National Public Radio.

I had the pleasure of working with an NPR station during my college years, KUT-FM in Austin, TX. We developed the Longhorn Radio Network to package public affairs programming for distribution to commercial radio stations. These shows helped stations to fulfill their public affairs commitment to the FCC.

Non-profit organizations and Industry producers provided public affairs programs to commercial radio stations around the country. They included "The NASA Report," "Genius on the Black Side," "Energy Tomorrow," "University Forum," "Healthcare Journal," "Here's to Veterans," "Nightbird & Company," "Voices of Vista," "William B. Williams & Company," "Country News" and "Guard Session."

Public Radio International, founded in 1983, is a media content provider to public radio stations. American Public Media, launched in 1994, is the second largest producer of public radio programs after NPR (its non-profit parent) and owns radio stations. APM is best known for the distribution for Garrison Keillor's "A Prairie Home Companion." The Public Radio Exchange, founded in 2003, is a non-profit web-based platform for digital distribution, review and licensing of programs for broadcast and Internet use.

Other public radio stations include campus, arts, ethnic stations and alternative stations.

Public Affairs Programming on Commercial TV

The major TV networks (CBS, NBC, ABC and Dumont) produced some public affairs shows in the 1950's and 1960's. They included "Omnibus," "See It Now," "Camera Three," "You Are There," "Take a Trip," "The American Forum," "Community Workshop" and others.

Some had educational content and were the genesis of distance learning, including "Sunrise Semester," "Ding Dong School," "Schools Are Your Business," "Reading For Teachers," "Operation Alphabet," "Mathematics For You," "Spin Top School."

Public affairs programs with news themes included "Great Decisions," "America Wants to Know" and "International Zone." Some are still on the air, including "Meet the Press," "Issues and Answers/This Week" and "Face the Nation."

Some of the Sunday shows had religious focus and were produced by faith based organizations and production companies. They included "This is the Life," "Look Up and Live," "Sacred Heart," "Lamp Unto My Feet," "The Christophers," "Directions," "Insight," "Frontiers of Faith," Davey and Goliath," "Jewish Hour" "Oral Roberts Show," "Christian Science" and "Catholic Hour." "Life is Worth Living" featuring Bishop Fulton J. Sheen, was a primetime ratings hit, competing against Milton Berle's NBC-TV variety show.

Industry groups produced shows that ran on local stations, including "The Big Picture," "This Interesting World," "Farm Front," "Your Government," "Americans at Work," "Let's Find Out" and "Industry on Parade" (from the National Association of Manufacturers).

Syndicated shows that were entertaining and fulfilled public affairs criteria included "Wild Kingdom with Marlin Perkins," "Joe DiMaggio's Dugout," "Johns Hopkins Review," "Dr. Spock," "Championship Bridge," "It's News to Me," "You Asked For It," "G.E. College Bowl," "Exploring" and "The Undersea World of Jacques Cousteau."

Public Television

Public Television traces its founding to 1952, as Educational Television and Radio Center (ETRC), by a grant from the Ford Foundation's Fund for Adult Education. It was a service for exchanging and distributing educational television programs produced by local television stations to other stations.

The first public TV station to sign on the air was KUHT in Houston, TX, in 1953. The second was KTHE in Los Angeles, CA, soon followed by WQED in Pittsburgh, PA, KQED in San Francisco, CA, and WTTW in Chicago, IL. Alabama ETV was the first state network.

ETRC began operating as a network in 1954. The initial programs were distributed on kinescope film to affiliated stations. The initial shows were comprised of on-air adult education. Early educational TV was the beginning of the distance learning movement. The organization moved from Ann Arbor, MI, to New York City in 1958 and changed its name to the National Educational Television and Radio Center (NETRC).

Distance learning education and university courses have a history that predated television. In 1728, the first correspondence course ran an ad in the Boston Gazette. In 1873, the first correspondence schools were offered by The Society to Encourage Studies at Home. In 1892, the University of Chicago was the first traditional educational institution in the U.S. to offer correspondence courses. In 1906, primary schools followed suit.

In 1922, radio broadcasting became a viable means of transmitting information, and Pennsylvania State College began broadcasting courses over the radio. In 1925, State University of Iowa began offering course credit for radio broadcast courses. In 1953, KUHT-TV, the first educational TV station in the United States, offered televised college classes for credit. In 1965, the University of Wisconsin began a statewide educational program for physicians in a telephone-based format. In 1976, the first "virtual college" with no physical campus was in operation, Coastline Community College, offering tele-courses.

NET began acquiring programming from the BBC in the U.K. in 1959. These imported shows became a staple of public television, later inspiring original American programming produced by affiliated stations.

In 1963, the name was shortened to NET, and the radio assets were spun off, eventually becoming known as NPR. The Corporation for Public Broadcasting (CPB) was founded in 1967, putting dozens more educational TV stations on the air. Conventional wisdom was that having the stations being on the air would improve school system standards.

The Public Broadcasting Service (PBS) first began operations in 1969, and on October 5, 1970, PBS officially began broadcasting. Programs that began their runs on NET, such as "Washington Week" and "Sesame Street," continue to air on PBS today.

The 1950s were the innovative years of commercial television, and key elements were later integrated into public TV, notably live drama, musical specials and documentaries.

One of those innovations was "Omnibus," a live arts and drama anthology, aired by CBS-TV on Sunday afternoons and hosted by Alistair Cooke. This introduced Cooke to America, and he later hosted the longtime PBS drama anthology "Masterpiece Theatre."

Commercial TV had the live drama series such as "Westinghouse Studio One," "Kraft TV Theatre," "The U.S. Steel Hour," "Playhouse 90," "Alcoa-Goodyear Theatre," "Ford Theatre," "Hallmark Hall of Fame," "Lux Video Theatre," "General Electric Theatre" (hosted by Ronald Reagan) and "Suspense."

Into those footsteps came public TV with "Play of the Week." The premiere broadcast was "Medea," Oct. 12, 1959, starring Judith Anderson, Aline MacMahon and Coleen Dewhurst. Major Broadway and Hollywood stars appeared on the drama shows at union scale, out of their desire to stimulate the arts on the new medium of TV.

Other "Play of the Week" highlights included "The World of Sholom Aleichem," 1959, stories by the Yiddish writer, starring Gertrude Berg, Sam Levene, Zero Mostel, Nancy Walker, Lee Grant, Morris Carnovsky, Jack Gilford, Charlotte Rae. "Highlights of New Faces," 1960, was a musical-comedy starring Paul Lynde, Alice Ghostley, Robert Clary. "The Iceman Cometh," 1960, starred Jason Robards, Robert Redford, Myron McCormick, James Broderick.

Also on "Play of the Week" were "Two Plays by William Saroyan," 1960, starred Walter Matthau, Orson Bean, Larry Hagman, Eddie Hodges, Myron McCormick. "New York Scrapbook," 1961, starred Orson Bean and Kaye Ballard. "The Master Builder," 1961, starred E.G. Marshall and Phyllis Love. "The Star Wagon," 1966, starred Dustin Hoffman, Orson Bean, Eileen Brennan.

The PBS drama anthology became known in the 1970s as "Hollywood Television Theatre." It premiered with "The Andersonville Trial," 1970, directed by George C. Scott, and starred Richard Basehart, William Shatner, Martin

Sheen, Buddy Ebsen, Cameron Mitchell, Jack Cassidy, Michael Burns, Alan Hale, Charles McGraw.

Also on "Hollywood Television Theatre" were "Trail of Tears," 1970, starred Jack Palance, Johnny Cash, Pat Hingle, Kent Smith, June Carter Cash. "The Typists," 1971, starred Eli Wallach and Anne Jackson. "Scarecrow," 1972, covered the Salem Witch Trials and starred Blythe Danner, Gene Wilder, Nina Foch, Will Geer, Pete Duel, Norman Lloyd, Peter Kastner. "Carola," 1973, starred Leslie Caron, Mel Ferrer, Anthony Zerbe. "The Last of Mrs. Lincoln," 1976, starred five-time Tony Awards winner Julie Harris recreating her stage role about Mary Todd Lincoln, the misunderstood U.S. First Lady.

Another series was "Theatre in America." "June Moon," 1974, starred Jack Cassidy, Susan Sarandon, Estelle Parsons, Kevin McCarthy, Stephen Sondheim (in his acting debut). "Double Solitaire," 1974, starred Richard Crenna, Susan Clark, Harold Gould. "For the Use of the Hall," 1975, directed by Lee Grant, starred Susan Anspach, Barbara Barrie, David Hedison, Joyce Van Patten. "The Year of the Dragon," 1975, starred George Takei and Pat Suzuki. "Out of Our Fathers' House," 1978, starred Dianne Wiest and Carol Kane.

Then came "Masterpiece Theatre," importing some of the finest dramas from the BBC. Popular series in the long run of the show have included "Poirot," "Downton Abbey," "The First Churchills," "House of Cards, "I, Claudius," "American Family: Journey of Dreams," "Brideshead Revisited," "The Jewel and the Crown," "Mr. Selfridge," "Indian Summers," the Jane Austen series, "Tales of Charles Dickens," "Poldark," "The Duchess of Duke Street," "Jeeves and Wooster," "Sherlock," "Prime Suspect," "Agatha Christie's Miss Marple" and "The Inspector Lynley Mysteries." The first host of "Masterpiece Theatre" was Alistair Cooke, who had previously hosted the cultural series "Omnibus" on CBS-TV and the documentary series "America" on NBC-TV.

Public TV also brought us "American Playhouse." "I Never Sang for My Father," 1988, starred Daniel J. Travanti, Harold Gould, Dorothy McGuire. "Zora is My Name," 1990, starred Ruby Dee, Lou Gossett, Flip Wilson, Beau Richards, Paula Kelly. "Cats," 1998, starred Elaine Paige, John Mills. "Merry Christmas, George Bailey," 1999, was a recreated radio drama, from "Lux Playhouse" 1947 staging of "It's a Wonderful Life" and starred Sally Field, Bill Pullman, Martin Landau, Penelope Ann Miller, Jerry Van Dyke, Joseph Mantagna, Christian Slater, Nathan Lane, Carol Kane, Robert Guillaume, Casey Kasem. "The Man Who Came to Dinner," 2000, starred Nathan Lane and Jean Smart. "A Streetcar Named Desire," 2001, was the operatic version of Tennessee Williams' Pulitzer Prize-winning play and starred Renee Fleming, Elizabeth Putral and the San Francisco Opera, with original music by Andre Previn and Philip Littell. "Gin Game," 2003, starred Dick Van Dyke and Mary Tyler Moore.

The PBS popular shows have included "The French Chef," hosted by Julia Child, "Wall Street Week," "Nova," "The Firing Line with William F. Buckley," "Great Performances," "The Charlie Rose Show," "The Lehrer-MacNeill Hour," "The American Experience," "American Masters," "Bill Moyers' Journal," "Meeting of the Minds" (with Steve Allen), "Nature," "Austin City Limits," "History Detectives," "This Old House," "Kaleidoscope," "Antiques Roadshow," "Soundstage," "The Joy of Painting" and "Frontline."

Popular British TV series have been on the PBS schedule since the 1960s, including "Upstairs, Downstairs," "The Forsyte Saga," "Fawlty Towers," "Are You Being Served," "BBC World News," "Doctor Who," "Horizon Nature," "Monty Python's Flying Circus," "An Age of Kings," "The Benny Hill Show," "Keeping Up Appearances," "Red Dwarf," "Mr. Bean" and "The Eastenders."

PBS supported the production of landmark American original shows such as "The Scarlet Letter," "The Civil War," "The Adams Chronicles," "The Great American Dream Machine" and the Ken Burns documentary mini-series.

On-air fund-raising became entertaining programming for PBS stations, including auctions and pledge drives. Complimenting those have been the motivational specials, golden oldies concerts and theatrical spectaculars. Very little of PBS' funding comes from government. Credit must be paid to the supporting foundations, corporations and "Viewers Like You."

Children's Shows on TV

Television became the window on the world for Baby Boomer children. The TV set was the babysitter in an era where both parents worked outside the home. It was also the source of education and inspiration for kids.

The first kid shows were live participation series. "Howdy Doody" set the tone for the TV industry, with its Peanut Gallery of kids, the likeable Buffalo Bob Smith as the host, puppet Howdy Doody as the kid hero, Clarabell the Clown and a cast of characters in the mythical village of Doodyville.

The success of Howdy Doody spawned many other series for kids and with kids as participants. These included "The Paul Winchell & Jerry Mahoney Show," "Kukla, Fran & Ollie" (Burr Tillstrom, Fran Allison), "The Quiz Kids," "Super Circus," "Rootie Kazootie," "The Pinky Lee Show" (starring a former burlesque comic who later inspired Pee Wee Herman), "The Soupy Sales Show," "Andy's Gang" (Andy Devine), "The Gumby Show," "Shari Lewis Show," "The Magic Land of Allakazam" (Mark Wilson) and "Beany and Cecil."

There were shows filled with entertainment but also teaching messages. "Watch Mr. Wizard" featured Don Herbert teaching science experiments to kids in the studio. "Ding Dong School" was hosted by Dr. Frances Horwich. The biggest was "Captain Kangaroo," hosted by Robert Keeshan, who had previously played Clarabell the Clown on "The Howdy Doody Show."

Into the realm of children's programming came public TV in the late 1960s. Fred Rogers hosted "Mister Rogers' Neighborhood," first on Pittsburgh TV, then on Canadian TV and mostly on PBS. "Sesame Street" has been running on PBS since 1969, produced by the Children's Television Workshop, featuring music, comedy, education and a host of guest stars. Sesame spawned other PBS shows, including "The Electric Company," "Zoom," "Newton's Apple," "Barney and Friends," "Dragon Tales," "Teletubbies," "Cailou," "Clifford the Big Red Dog," "Arthur," "Dinosaur Train," "Curious George," "Rosie and Jim," "DragonflyTV," "Tots TV" and "Peg+Cat."

With the advent of cable TV, the systems were obligated to give channel space for public access TV stations. Some are operated by non-profit foundations, others by city municipalities and others by academic institutions. These channels feature speeches, coverage of community events, televised forums and other elements of interest to communities. Some have played documentaries and student produced programming. Cable TV's contribution to public affairs has included community events, such as recognizing local heroes.

The cable era brought audiences Nickelodeon. It started in 1977 as Pinwheel and changed in 1979 to Nickelodeon. Nick's popular shows included "SpongeBob SquarePants," "Mr. Wizard's World," "Clarissa Explains It All," "Teenage Mutant Ninja Turtles," "The Ren and Stimpy Show," "Are You Afraid of the Dark," "The Fairly Odd Parents," "Dora the Explorer," "Power Rangers," "I-Carly," "Jimmy Neutron," "Degrassi," "Johnny Bravo" and "Blues Clues." Since 1985, it has shared its channel space with Nick at Nite, showing classic TV reruns, in turn spawning TV Land, Nick Jr. and Teen Nick.

The cable era brought the designation E/I, standing for entertainment and information. The Discovery Channel and Animal Planet focused upon nature and wildlife. The Science and National Geographic Channels brought documentaries and instructional programming to commercial TV.

Running E/I shows gave cable the opportunity to program educational and children's shows, usually on Saturday and Sunday mornings. Other cable channels run shows such as "Mystery Hunters," "Better Planet TV," "Animal Atlas," "Wonderful World," "Lucky Dog," "Missing Cold Cases," "Awesome Adventures," "Dog Whisperer," "Henry Ford's Innovation" and "Teen Kids News."

The internet has the opportunity to feature public service and community affairs content. There exist online websites, blogs, volunteer forums, chat rooms and sources to promote community events.

Social media often provides outlets to educate the public, promote causes, publicize community events and enlist citizens in volunteering initiatives.

I'd like to see corporate websites offer space to causes that they champion. They could publicize events and initiatives in communities in which they do business. They could acknowledge employees who serve the community. This could make web based embracement of worthy causes possible.

*Public television memories, including pledge drives and auctions,
Alistair Cooke hosting "Masterpiece Theatre," cultural drama,
William F. Buckley hosting "The Firing Line" and documentaries.*

Joan Ganz Cooney, executive producer of "Sesame Street,"
received the Presidential Medal of Freedom, the nation's
highest civilian honor, in 1995 from President Bill Clinton.

Chapter 16

STRATEGIES FOR NON-PROFIT ORGANIZATIONS

The Art of Learning From Failure to Get Better

Success is just in front of our faces. Yet, we often fail to see it coming. Too many companies live with their heads in the sand. Many go down into defeat because it was never on their radar to change.

A colleague recently complained about her corporation: "Things are much the same at this company, and I don't see much changing unless leadership does."

The answer is that companies need not roll over and accept less than the best. And yes, it takes courage to get management unstuck in their ways. 92% of all problems in organizations stem from poor management decisions.

The biggest mistakes which many of have made:

1. Abilities and Talents:
   - Making the same mistakes more than twice, without studying the mitigating factors.
   - Taking incidents out of context and mis-diagnosing situations.

- Rationalizing occurrences, after the fact.
- Appearing self-contained, therefore precluding others from wanting to help me.
- Inability to cultivate other people's support of me at the times that I needed it most.

2. Resources:
   - Attempting projects without the proper resources to do the job well.
   - Not knowing people with sufficient pull and power. Thinking that friends would help introduce me or help network to key influential people.
   - Failure to effective networking techniques early enough in my career path.
   - Inability to finely develop the powers of people participating in the networking process.

3. Other People:
   - Accepting people at their words without questioning.
   - Showing proper respect to other people and assuming that they would show or were capable of showing comparable respect to others.
   - Doing favors for others without asking anything in return, if I expected quid pro quo at a later time. Not telling people what I wanted and then being disappointed that they did not read minds or deliver favors of their own volition.
   - Befriending people who were too needy, always taking without offering to reciprocate. Continuing to feed their needs, a one-way relationship.
   - Picking the wrong causes to champion at the wrong times and with insufficient resources.
   - Working with the false assumption that people want and need comparable things. Incorrectly assuming that all would pursue their agendas fairly. A better understanding of personality types, human motivations and behavioral factors would have provided insight to handle situations on a customized basis.

- Offering highly creative ideas and brain power to those who could not grasp their brilliance...especially to those who were fishing for free ideas they could then market as their own.

4. Circumstances Beyond Our Control:
   - Working with equipment, resources and people from a source without my standards of quality control...trying to make the best of bad situations.
   - Changing trends, upon which I could not capitalize but which others could.

5. False Calculations:
   - Incorrectly estimating the time and resources necessary to do something well.
   - Getting blindsided because I did not do enough research.
   - Failure to plan sufficiently ahead, at the right times.
   - Setting sights too low. Not thinking big enough.

6. Timing:
   - Offering advice before it was solicited.
   - Feeling pressured to offer solutions before diagnosing situations properly.
   - Not thinking of enough angles and possibilities...sooner.

7. Marketplace-External Factors:
   - Not reading the opportunities soon enough.
   - Not being able to spot, create or capitalize upon emerging trends at their beginnings.

8. Stages of Mistakes:
   - Discovering errors (sensory-motor, sounds-language and logical selection).
   - Recognizing mistakes.
   - Separating successful elements from failures we do not need to duplicate.
   - Learning from mistakes.
   - Learning from success.

- Mentoring yourself and others toward a higher stream of knowledge.
- The wisdom that comes from making mistakes, comprehending their outcomes, and developing a knowledge base to achieve success.

9. Gradations of Failing:
   - Not seeing the warning signs.
   - Distinguishing among friends, enemies and the majority group, those who could care less about you but who will tap whatever resources available to get their needs met.
   - Never seeing victories as quite enough.
   - Feeling that someone else wins when you fail.
   - Repeating self-defeating behaviors.
   - Holding unrealistic viewpoints.
   - Thinking that you never fail, that failing is for other people and organizations.

Learning the stumbling blocks of failure prepares one to attain true success. Fear is the biggest contributor to failure, and it can be a motivator for success. You cannot make problems go away, simply by ignoring that they exist.

Everybody fails at things for which they are not suited. The process of learning what one is best suited to do is not a failure…it is a great success. Learn from the best and the worst. People who make the biggest bungling mistakes are showing you pitfalls to avoid.

Many of us make the same mistakes over and over again. That is to be expected and teaches us volumes, preparing us for success. There is no plan that is fool-proof. One plans, learns, reviews and plans further.

One learns three times more from failure than success. One learns three times more clearly when witnessing and analyzing the failures of others they know or have followed. History teaches us about cycles, trends, misapplications of resources, wrong approaches and vacuums of thought. People must apply history to their own lives. If we document our own successes, then these case studies will make us more successful in the future.

Understanding Figures and What They Symbolize, Relating Directly to Your Business Success.

Business bases much of what it does on statistics. Most often, they're financial numbers or sales goals. More importantly are the Big Picture statistics that affect every aspect of business growth and success. The way in which the bigger issues are interpreted has direct bearing on strategy and implementation.

Here are some of the most significant statistics that relate to your ability to do business:

Only 2% of organizations have a plan of any kind. What many of them think is a plan include some accounting figures or sales goals. That is not a full-scope plan. Of the companies who continue to operate without a plan, 40% of them will be out of business in the next 10 years.

Only 2% of those who call themselves consultants really are just that. That 2% includes all the doctors, lawyers, accountants and engineers...those of us who actually advise. Most so-called consultants are vendors who peddle what they have to sell, rather than what the client companies really need. The answer is for companies to utilize seasoned advisers, rather than coaches and other vendors.

Research shows that change is 90% positive and beneficial. Why, then, do many organizations fight what is in their best interest? The average person and organization changes 71% per year. The mastery of change is to benefit from it, rather than become a victim of it.

92% of all business mistakes may be attributed to poor management decisions. 85% of the time, a formal program of crisis preparedness will help the organization to avert the crisis. The average person spends 150 hours each year in looking for misplaced information and files. One learns three times more from failure than from success. Failures are the surest tracks toward future successes.

One-third of the Gross National Product is sent each year toward cleaning up mistakes, rework, make-goods, corrective action and correcting defects. Yet, only 5.1% is spent on education, which is the key to avoiding mistakes on the front end.

50% of the population reads books. 50% do not. Of all high school graduates, 37% will never read another book after formal schooling. Of all college graduates, 16% will never read another book. Thus, a declining overall level of education in our society and serious challenges faced by organizations in training the workforce. Yet, the holdings of the world's libraries are doubling every 14 years.

Today's work force requires three times the amount of training they now get in order to remain competitive in the future. 29% of the work force wants their boss' job. 70% of corporate CEOs think that business is too much focused on the short-term.

The human brain has more than 300 million component parts. The human brain connects to 13 billion nerves in the body. The human body has 600 muscles. The human body has 206 bones. The average person speaks 30,000 words per day. The average person is bombarded with more than 600 messages per day. More enlightened, actively communicating people are bombarded with more than 900 messages per day.

98% of all new business starts are small businesses. 45% of small business owners are children of small business owners. 83% of all domestic companies have fewer than 20 employees. Only 7% of all companies have 100 or more employees.

The current success rate for organizational hires is 14%. If further research is put into looking at the total person and truly fitting the person to the job, then the success rate soars to 75%. That involves testing and more sophisticated hiring practices.

Retaining good employees, involving training, motivation and incentives, is yet another matter. According to research conducted by the Ethics Resource Center:

- Employees of organizations steal 10 times more than do shoplifters.
- Employee theft and shoplifting accounting for 15% of the retail cost of merchandise.
- 35% of employees steal from the company.
- 28% of those who steal think that they deserve what they take.
- 21% of those who steal think that the boss can afford the losses.
- 56% of employees lie to supervisors.

- 41% of employees falsify records and reports.
- 31% of the workforce abuses substances.

On any given day, Americans spend $33 million buying lottery tickets. On that same day, 99 American families fall below the poverty line. 68% of Americans do not like to take chances. 5% of all Americans go to McDonald's every day.

99% of American women think that contributing to or bettering society is important. 35% of Americans are involved in community service and charity activities. During the last 3,500 years, the world has been at peace only 8 percent of the time.

Data from the Census Bureau shows that 69% of new companies with employees survive at least two years, and that 51% survive at least five years. An independent analysis by the Bureau of Labor Statistics shows that 49% of new businesses survive for five years or more. 34% of new businesses survive ten years or more, and 26% are still in business at least 15 years after being started.

Small businesses really do drive the economy. Many people believe that businesses frequently fail because there are a large number closing every year. In 2009, for example, more than 550,000 businesses were opened, and more than 660,000 closed. This occurred during a recession. However, during an economic expansion, the number of new businesses would outnumber the closures.

Many people may not realize how many small businesses there are in the country. In 2011, the Department of Commerce estimated that there were 27.5 million businesses in the United States. Only 18,000 of those businesses had more than 500 employees, and the rest were considered small businesses.

29% are still in business at the end of year 10. And the biggest drop comes in the first 5 years, when half of startups go belly up. This shows that the odds are against startups staying in business. The internet home business success rate is only 5%.

Avoid the Tired, Trite Terms.
Encourage Original Thought. Focus on Priorities and Strategy.

Words count. Put together, they reflect corporate culture. Used out of context, words become excuses, gibberish, rationalizations and wastes of energy.

When people hear certain words and expressions often enough, they parrot them. Rather than use critical thinking to communicate, many people often gravitate to the same old tired catch phrases.

I sat in a meeting of highly educated business executives. The presenter was dropping the term "brand" into every other sentence. The word had lost its power and came across as a fill-in-the-blank substitution for a more appropriate though. Many people used to do the same thing with the word "technology," using it far from its reasonable definitions.

These clichés do not belong in business dialog, in strategic planning and in corporate strategy. These expressions are trite and reflect a copy-cat way of talking and thinking:

"Solutions" is a tired 1990's term, taken from technology hype. People who use it are vendors, selling what they have to solve your "problems," rather than diagnosing and providing what your company needs. It is a misnomer to think that a quick fix pawned off as a "solution" will take care of a problem once and for all. Such a word does not belong in conversation and business strategy, let alone the name of the company.

The "brand" is a marketing term. The strategy, culture and vision are many times greater and more important.

In the 1960's, TV sitcom writers began every scene with "So..." After enough years of hearing it, people lapse that dialog into corporate conversations. It is intended to reduce the common denominator of the discussion to that of the questioner. It is monotonous, and there are more creative ways to engage others into conversation aside from minimizing the dialog.

"Value proposition" is a sales term and is one-sided toward the person offering it. It implies that the other side must buy in without question.

"Right now" is a vendor term for what they're peddling, rather than what the marketplace really needs. Expect to render good business all the time.

"Customer care" means that customer service is palmed off on some call center. "Customer experience" comes right out of marketing surveys, which rarely ask for real feedback or share the findings with company decision makers. That is so wrong, as customer service must be every person's responsibility. Service should not be something that is sold but which nurtures client relationships.

Many of these stock phrases represent "copywriting" by people who don't know about corporate vision. Their words overstate, get into the media and are accepted by audiences as fact. Companies put too much of their public persona in the hands of marketers and should examine more closely the partial images which they put into the cyberspace. Our culture hears and believes the hype, without looking beyond the obvious.

Here are some examples of the misleading and misrepresenting things one sees and hears in the Information Age. These terms are judgmental and should not be used in marketing, least of all in business strategy: Easy, Better, Best, For all your needs, Perfection, Number one, Good to go, Results, World class, Hearts and minds, Cool, The end of the day, Virtual, Right now, Not so much and Game changing.

Street talk, misleading slogans and terms taken out of context do not belong in the business vocabulary. Business planning requires insightful thinking and language which clearly delineates what the company mission is and how it will grow.

These are the characteristics of effective words, phrases and, thus, company philosophy:

- Focus upon the customer.
- Honor the employees.
- Define business as a process, not a quick fix.
- Portray their company as a contributor, not a savior.
- Clearly defines their niche.
- Say things that inspire you to think.
- Compatible with other communications.
- Remain consistent with their products, services and track record.

Chapter 17

COLLABORATIONS, PARTNERING AND JOINT-VENTURING

The biggest source of growth and increased opportunities in today's business climate lie in the way that individuals and companies work together.

It is becoming increasingly rare to find an individual or organization that has not yet been required to team with others. Lone rangers and sole-source providers simply cannot succeed in competitive environments and global economies. Those who benefit from collaborations, rather than become the victim of them, will log the biggest successes in business years ahead.

Just as empowerment, team building and other processes apply to formal organizational structures, then teams of independents can likewise benefit from the concepts. There are rules of protocol that support and protect partnerships…having a direct relationship to those who profit most from teamwork.

Definitions of these three terms will help to differentiate their intended objectives:

Collaborations: Parties willingly cooperating together. Working jointly with others, especially in an intellectual pursuit. Cooperation with an instrumentality with which one is not immediately connected.

Partnering: A formal relationship between two or more associates. Involves close cooperation among parties, with each having specified and joint rights and responsibilities.

Joint-Venturing: Partners come together for specific purposes or projects that may be beyond the scope of individual members. Each retains individual identity. The joint-venture itself has its own identity, reflecting favorably upon work to be done and upon the partners.

Here are some examples of Collaborations:

- Parties and consultants involved in taking a company public work together as a team.
- Niche specialists collectively conduct a research study or performance review.
- Company turnaround situation requires a multi-disciplinary approach.
- A group of consultants offer their collective talents to clients on a contract basis.
- The client is opening new locations in new communities and asks its consultants to formulate a plan of action and oversee operating aspects.
- Professional societies and associations.
- Teams of health care professionals, as found in clinics and hospitals.
- Composers and lyricists to write songs.
- Artists of different media creating festivals, shows and museums.
- Advocate groups for causes.
- Communities rallying around certain causes (crime, education, drug abuse, literacy, youth activities, etc.).
- Libraries and other repositories of information and knowledge.
- Here are some examples of Partnering:
- Non-competing disciplines create a new mousetrap, based upon their unique talents, and collectively pursue new marketplace opportunities.

- Manufacturing companies team with retail management experts to open a string of widget stores.
- A formal rollup or corporation to provide full-scope professional service to customers.
- Non-profit organizations banning resources for programs or fundraising.
- Institutions providing startup or expansion capital.
- Managing mergers, acquisitions and divestitures.
- Procurement and purchasing capacities.
- Corporations working with public sector and non-profit organizations to achieve mutual goals in the communities.
- Private sector companies doing privatized work for public sector entities.
- Organ donor banks and associations, in consortium with hospitals.
- Vendors, trainers, computer consultants and other consultants who strategically team with clients to do business. Those who don't help to develop the business on the front end are just vendors and subcontractors.
- Here are some examples of Joint-Venturing:
- Producers of energy create an independent drilling or marketing entity.
- An industry alliance creates a lobbying arm or public awareness campaign.
- Multiple companies find that doing business in a new country is easier when a consortium operates.
- Hardware, software and component producers revolutionizing the next generation of technology.
- Scientists, per research program.
- Educators, in the creation and revision of curriculum materials.
- Distribution centers and networks for retail products.
- Aerospace contractors and subcontractors with NASA.
- Telecommunications industry service providers.
- Construction industry general contractors, subcontractors and service providers in major building projects.
- Group marketing programs, such as auto dealer clusters, municipalities for economic development, travel and tourism destinations, trade association and product image upgrades.

- International trade development, including research, marketing, relocation, negotiations and lobbying.

Situations Which Call for Teams to Collaborate

1. Business Characteristics: Most industries and core business segments cannot be effectively served by one specialty. It is imperative that multiple disciplines within the core business muster their resources.

2. Circumstances: People get thrown together by necessity and sometimes by accident. They are not visualized as a team and often start at cross-purposes. Few participants are taught how to best utilize each other's respective expertise. Through osmosis, a working relationship evolves.

3. Economics: In today's downsized business environment, outsourcing, privatization and consortiums are fulfilling the work. Larger percentages of contracts are awarded each year to those who exemplify and justify their team approaches. Those who solve business problems and predict future challenges will be retained. Numerically, collaboration contracts are more likely to be renewed.

4. Demands of the Marketplace: Savvy business owners know that no one supplier can "do it all." Accomplished managers want teams that give value-added, create new ideas and work effectively. Consortiums must continually improve, in order to justify investments.

5. Desire to Create New Products and Services: There are only four ways to grow one's business: (1) sell more products-services, (2) cross-sell existing customers, (3) create new products-services and (4) joint-venture to create new opportunities. #3 and 4 cannot be accomplished without teaming with others.

6. Opportunities to Be Created: Once one makes the commitment to collaborate, circumstances will define the exact teaming structures. The best opportunities are created.

7. Strong Commitment Toward Partnering: Those of us who have collaborated with other professionals and organizations know the value. Once one sees the profitability and creative injections, then one aggressively advocates the teaming processes. It is difficult to work in

a vacuum thereafter. Creative partnerships don't just happen and are creatively pursued.

This is what collaborations are NOT:

- Shrouds to get business, where subcontractors may later be found to do the work.
- Where one partner presents the work of others as their own.
- Where one party misrepresents his-her capabilities, in such a way as to overshadow the promised team approach.
- Where one partner treats others more like subcontractors or vendors.
- Where one participant keeps other collaborators away from the client's view.
- Ego fiefdoms, where one participant assumes a demeanor that harms the project.
- Where cost considerations preclude all partners from being utilized.
- Where one partner steals business from another.
- Where non-partners are given advantageous position over ground-floor members who paid the dues.
- Where one or more parties are knowingly used for their knowledge and then dismissed.
- These are the kinds of people and organizations who need to collaborate:
- Those who have not stopped learning and continue to acquire knowledge.
- Those who are good and wanting to get progressively better.
- Those who have captained other teams and, thus, know the value of being a good member of someone else's team.
- Those who do their best work in collaboration with others.
- Those who appreciate creativity and new challenges.
- Those who have been mentored and who mentor others.
- Those who don't want to rest upon their laurels.
- Those who appreciate fresh ideas, especially from unexpected sources.
- These are the kinds of people and organizations who do not want to collaborate:

- Those who have never had to collaborate, partner or joint-venture before.
- Those who don't believe in the concept and usually give nebulous reasons why.
- Those who think they're sufficiently trained and learned to conduct business.
- Those who want only to be the center of attention.
- Those who fear being compared to others of stature in their own right.
- Those who think that the marketplace may not buy the team approach.
- Those who are afraid that their process or expertise will not stand the test when compared with others.
- Those who had one or two bad experiences with partnering in the past, usually because they were on the periphery or really weren't equal partners in the first place.

These are the characteristics of an excellent collaborator:

Already has a sense of self-worth.

Has a bona fide track record on their own.

Have a commitment toward knowledge enhancement.

Walk the Talk by their interactions with others.

Supports collaborators in developing their own businesses, offering referrals.

Have been on other teams in the past, with case studies of actually collaborations.

Has a track record of successes and failures to their credit, with an understanding of the causal factors, outcomes and lessons learned.

Stages of Relationship Building for Partners

1. Want to Get Business: Seeking rub-off effect, success by association. Sounds good to the marketplace. Nothing ventured, nothing gained. Why not try!

2. Want to Garner Ideas: Learn more about the customer. Each team member must commit to professional development, taking the program

to a higher level. Making sales calls (mandated or voluntarily) does not constitute relationship building.

3. First Attempts: Conduct programs that get results, praise, requests for more. To succeed, it needs to be more than an advertising and direct marketing campaign.

4. Mistakes, Successes & Lessons: Competition, marketplace changes or urgent need led the initiative to begin. Customer retention and enhancement program requires a cohesive team approach and multiple talents.

5. Continued Collaborations: Collaborators truly understand teamwork and had prior successful experiences at customer service. The sophisticated ones are skilled at building and utilizing colleagues and outside experts.

6. Want and advocate teamwork: Team members want to learn from each other. All share risks equally. Early successes inspire deeper activity. Business relationship building is considered an ongoing process, not a "once in awhile" action or marketing gimmick.

7. Commitment to the concept and each other: Each team member realizes something of value. Customers recommend and freely refer business to the institution. What benefits one partner benefits all.

Evaluating Collective Working Relationships

- I have observed the greatest successes with collaborations, partnering and joint-ventures to occur when:
- Crisis or urgent need forced the client to hire a consortium.
- Time deadlines and nature of the project required a cohesive team approach.
- The work required multiple professional skills.
- Consortium members were tops in their fields.
- Consortium members truly understood teamwork and had prior successful experiences in joint-venturing.
- Consortium members wanted to learn from each other.
- Early successes spurred future collaborations.

- Joint-venturing was considered an ongoing process, not a "once in awhile" action.
- Each team member realized something of value.
- The client recommended the consortium to others.
- My own disappointments with previous collaborations include:
- Failure of participants to understand—and thus utilize—each other's talents.
- One or more participants have had one or a few bad experiences and tend to over-generalize about the worth of consortiums.
- One partner puts another down on the basis of academic credentials or some professional designation that sets themselves apart from other team members.
- Participants exhibit the "Lone Ranger" syndrome, preferring the comfort of trusting the one person they have counted upon.
- Participants exhibit the "I can do that" syndrome, thinking that they do the same exact things that other consortium members do and, thus, see no value in working together, sharing projects and referring business.
- Junior associates of consortium members want to hoard the billing dollars in-house, to look good to their superiors, enhance their billable quotas or fulfill other objectives that they are not sophisticated enough to identify.
- Junior associates of consortium members refuse to recognize seniority and wisdom of senior associates, utilizing the power of the budget to control creative thoughts and strategic thinking of subcontractors.

Here are the reasons to give the concepts of Collaborating, Partnering and Joint-Venturing a chance:

Think of the ones that got away, the opportunities that a team could have created. Think of contracts that were awarded to others who exhibited a team approach. Learn from industries where consortiums are the rule, rather than the exception (space, energy, construction, high-tech, etc.).

The marketplace is continually changing. Subcontractor, supplier, support talent and vendor information can be shared. Consortiums are inevitable. If we don't do it early, others will beat us to it.

The benefits for participating principals and firms include: Ongoing association and professional exchange with the best in respective fields. Utilize professional synergy to create opportunities that individuals could not. Serve as a beacon for professionalism. Provide access to experts otherwise not known to potential clients. Through demands uncovered, develop programs and materials to meet markets.

These are the truisms of collaborations, partnering and joint-ventures: Whatever measure you give will be the measure that you get back. The joy is in the journey, not in the final destination. The best destinations are not pre-determined in the beginning, but they evolve out of circumstances.

A body of work doesn't just happen. It's the culmination of a thoughtful, dedicated process…carefully strategized from some point forward. The objective is to begin that strategizing point sooner rather than later.

Chapter 18

COMMUNICATIONS PROGRAMS
FOR NON-PROFIT ORGANIZATIONS

I n many professions, the idea of full-scope, sophisticated positioning has been foreign up until now. Business development has occurred primarily by accident or through market demand.

Because of economic realities and the increased numbers of firms providing comparable services, the notion of business development is now a necessity, rather than a luxury.

Competition for customers-clients is sharpening. The professions are no longer held on a pedestal, a condition which mandates them to portray or enhance public images.

As companies adjust comfort levels and acquire confidence in the arena of business development, there is a direct relationship to billings, client mix diversity, market share, competitive advantage, stock price and levels of business which enable other planned growth.

Public perceptions are called "credence goods" by economists. Every organization must educate outside publics about what they do and how they do it.

This holds for corporate operating units and departments. You must always educate corporate opinion makers on how you function and the skill with which you operate.

Gaining confidence is crucial, as business relationships with professionals are established to be long-term in duration.

Each organization or should determine and craft its own character and personality, seeking to differentiate from others. That appeals to professionals within your own staff, those professionals whom your firm would like to attract and clients.

Top management must endorse corporate imaging and other forms of practice development, if your company is to grow and prosper. Few companies can even sustain present levels of sales without some degree of business development.

Some people in your organization will devote much time to promotions, public relations, marketing and advertising. This quality should be recognized and rewarded, since professionals with a sense of business direction play an important part in company growth.

Be it a "necessary evil" or not, corporate imaging activity can be accomplished with skill and success, provided that organizations follow the advice of professional communicators.

Non-profit organizations must maintain a delicate balance between seeking new business, replacing lost clients and nurturing client relationships. Operating units and departments must schedule and follow a program to market their worth to their companies.

No matter what time allocation basis is selected by the organization, it is vital that some basis exists in writing and in execution.

The non-profit organization that evokes a caring image and backs it up with service will be more successful.

Essential Ingredients of a Non-Profit Communications Program

Public Relations Program
- Complete generic press kits.
- Guidelines on working with the media.

- Pointers on training staff and volunteers as media spokespersons.
- Company collateral literature system.
- Guidelines on arranging speeches, seminars and town hall meetings.
- Ways to improve local community and government relations.
- Opinion pieces and bylined articles on key topics, suitable for placing in local newspapers under local bylines.
- Formula press releases and features, which can be locally customized.
- Other components of a program which can and should be customized.

Marketing Program
- Sales support.
- Business development.
- Direct marketing.
- Indirect marketing.
- Advertising.
- Business-to-business promotions.
- Industry and professional marketing.
- Point-of-purchase materials.
- Collateral materials.

Communications Manual
- Overall Philosophy and Writing Style.
- Statements to Make Publicly.
- Letters.
- Forms.
- Customer Comment Cards.
- Customer Service Correspondence.
- Sales Manual.
- Graphics Standards.

Crisis Communications Plan
Literature and Audio Visual Programs Which Portray Company Image
Government Relations Program
Community Relations Program
Contingency Program for Specified and Unplanned Emergencies

The use of social media has become a major communications vehicle for non-profit organizations. They use it to communicate their services to clients and donors, through such mechanisms as:

- Alerting stakeholders to immediate needs.
- Interacting with the community on a near-daily basis.
- Educating the public on programs and services.
- Advertising volunteer opportunities.
- Thanking grantors and donors for their support.
- Tweeting the progress of events.
- Posting videos.
- Responding to emergencies.
- Informing volunteers.
- Communicating with stakeholders
- Bringing awareness to organizational mission.
- Telling human-interest stories.
- Conveying research and supporting documents.
- Providing a forum for comments.
- Building likes tend to increase awareness, understanding and support.
- Replacing other media outlets that have been lost.
- Facilitating on-line fund raising campaigns.
- Allowing for immediate acknowledgement of public support.
- Inviting contributions from community of stakeholders.

Social media sites include Facebook, Linkedin, Twitter, Google Plus, YouTube, Instagram, Pininterest and Vimeo

Many organizations have blog sites. They include posts of articles, photos, news releases, client testimonials and event reminders.

Working Effectively With the News Media

Non-profit issues are very newsworthy. It is proper for a business overview professional to be interviewed for expert opinion on a particular subject, where the media needs depth and insight.

As the spokesperson, you are the expert, regardless of the interviewer's viewpoint, knowledge, or attitude. You should expect to lead the discussion, make your points, and stick to the subject.

The skill is to do interviews in such a way as to establish your company as a credible resource that media can call upon again, when it needs information and opinion. Those organizations which are often quoted as experts are perceived in various circles as such.

Reporters are skilled writers, who know how to gather news. The process dictates that journalists develop credible sources of information.

Reporters are conscientious and are not "out to get" business people. Their job is to recognize news and to convey facts to the public, while the information is still newsworthy. Thus, media deadlines must be met and respected.

Valid resources foster a cooperative relationship with the news media. Organizations that are serious about their responsibility to the media seek and follow the counsel of corporate imaging professionals. Counsel will educate you on the media, the personalities involved, how to interface with media, and how to generate your own news and feature stories into their hands.

Speaking to the media is an obligation that every business has. The skill with which it is done will have recognition on your side.

Public recognition of your expertise is a bank of goodwill that you will need to later draw upon. Reputations are created over time, and expertise is communicated over a duration. Recognize that relationships with media are good to have and must be responsibly maintained over the years.

Every profession has an objective vantage point over business and the economy. When you think more globally (rather than technically), article and interview subject matter is abundant.

Here are some pointers on positioning yourself and your organization: Fully research the subject matter beyond the technical aspects of the core business. See your position as unique and possessing a quality business overview. Determine which audiences most need to hear your expertise. Determine which desired effects this time commitment will have. Create an after-market to further distribute the published results.

The following interview techniques will yield the best possible interview: Phrase comments in non-technical terms. Keep answers in the 30-second time frame. Be prepared to further elaborate. Know and cite applicable case studies. Keep focus on the subject matter.

Remember that you are the resource, and the interviewer is there to showcase your knowledge. Because you are a credible third-party expert, the media should hear enough to want to call you back. Your subject matter is not controversial. Don't dwell on negative interviews you may have heard. Go in and remain positive. Follow up all interviews with notes of thanks, offering your expertise again at some future time. Let colleagues hear and critique your interview. Never stop learning the techniques and polishing the presentation.

Speaking to the media is an obligation that every organization has. The skill with which it is done will have recognition on your side. Public recognition of your expertise is a bank of goodwill that you will need to later draw upon.

Carefully determine which areas in which you are both an expert and can be quoted. Develop writing expertise that fits your comfort level and areas of knowledge. Read the consumer press to see which companies get published most often. Mailing reprints is the most effective way to assure that people you want to see your articles are getting the opportunity.

Reputations are created over time, and expertise is communicated over time. Recognize that relationships with media are good to have and must be responsibly maintained over the years.

These are the ways to make the news:

- Tie in with news events of the day.
- Conduct a poll or survey.
- Issue a report or summary of facts. Issue and diagnose statistics.
- Arrange an interview.
- Arrange for a testimonial.
- Make an analysis or prediction.

- Deliver a speech (arrange, write, and cover).
- Announce an appointment or committee.
- Celebrate an anniversary.
- Make a statement on a subject of interest.
- Bring a celebrity or guest speaker from elsewhere.
- Make an award.
- Hold a contest.
- Stage a special event.
- Adopt national reports and surveys locally.
- Salute an institute or body of people.
- Inspect a project. Organize a tour.

It is news when it:

- Has never been done before and takes a novel or unusual twist.
- Relates to famous people.
- Directly affects large numbers of people.
- Involves conflict or mystery.
- Was considered confidential and is now made public.
- Is funny, romantic, or entertaining.

Chapter 19

NON-PROFIT LEGENDS, THE
AUTHOR'S PHOTO GALLERY

Hank Moore is pictured with Lady Bird Johnson in 1993, planning an environmental event. He is pictured in 1985 with Lee P. Brown, receiving a merit award during Police Week. He is pictured in 1989, receiving the Savvy Award for community leadership, along with TV news anchor Ron Stone and Sister Helem Gay, founder of the Mission of Yahweh.

Hank Moore is pictured with Muhammad Ali at a 1974 gala event for the Christian Rescue Mission. He is pictured in 1992 at the Leadership in Action Awards dinner, with NBC-TV anchor Jan Carson and Alberto Gonzalez, who later served as U.S. Attorney General.

Hank Moore is pictured with Hanh Tran, Neil Bush, Melissa Williams and Kofi Sarkodie at a 2014 gala event for the IWrite Literacy Organization.

Hank Moore is pictured at the 1985 Alley Theatre Gala Ball,
as the celebrity DJ and emcee.

Hank Moore is pictured at the 1989 awards luncheon for a school mentorship program, along with HISD Superintendent Dr. Joan Raymond and Roland Rodriguez. Hank is pictured at a 1973 charity gala with Maureen Reagan.

Hank Moore is pictured receiving a proclamation in 1987 from Houston Mayor Kathy Whitmire. Also in the picture are Jimmy Wynn, Tom Koppa and Tom Kennedy. Also pictured with Mayor Whitmire in 1989 to promote a political nostalgia gala for the American Diabetes Association.

Vital to living a great life is community leadership and volunteerism. When you win awards for it, that caps off the pride in serving others. Hank Moore received awards from the United Nations, United Way, Dewar's Profile, The Savvy Award, Headliner's Award, National Association for Community Leadership and the Lifetime Achievement Award from Volunteer Houston on May 15, 2015.

Hank Moore is pictured with Ken Ginn and Charlie Thorp at a 1989 conference for the United Way. The workbook that he prepared planted the seed for what became this book. Hank is pictured receiving hos first lifetime achievement award for community leadership, at a 1988 gala event in Cincinnati, Ohio.

Hank Moore was the featured speaker at the Asian Chamber of Commerce in 2015. He honored community legends Linda Toyota, Felix Fraga, Martha Wong, Glen Gondo, Beth Wolff, Dan Parsons and Catherine A. Le.

"It's good business to help colleges"

"Our colleges and universities must have enormous quantities of new money almost constantly if they are to be enabled to serve society as it needs to be served. Every business institution benefits today from the money and labors that those now dead have put into the building of these institutions. We are all dependent upon them for future numbers of educated young men and women from which to choose, and for the continued expansion of man's knowledge of the world he inhabits.

"We owe these institutions a great debt, and we can pay this debt in two ways: By supporting them generously with contributions of money and time, and by upholding their freedom to remain places of open discussion, and to pursue truth wherever it is to be found.

"Last year our company contributed to colleges and universities more than $310,000 which represented 1.2% of profit before tax."

**J. Irwin Miller, Chairman
Cummins Engine Company**

A major problem in the education of students is rising costs. If companies wish to insure the availability of college talent, they must help support colleges with financial aid.

SPECIAL TO CORPORATE OFFICERS — A new booklet of particular interest if your company has not yet established an aid-to-education program. Write for: "How to Aid Education — and Yourself", Box 36, Times Square Station, New York, N.Y. 10036

COLLEGE IS BUSINESS' BEST FRIEND

Published as a public service in cooperation with The Advertising Council and the Council for Financial Aid to Education

Yes, I am interested in AIR FORCE EXPERIENCE (Check One) I understand there is no obligation.

After High School
☐ Experience, Technical Training (Age 17-27).

College Bound
☐ ROTC (Age 16-28). ☐ Academy (Age 17-21).

College Graduate
☐ Officer Training School (Max. age 29½).

Part-Time Challenge
☐ Reserve (Age 17-34).

Send Information ☐ Contact Me Immediately ☐
Prior Military Experience? YES ☐ NO ☐
If you checked ROTC, list colleges you plan to attend.

Name _____ Sex M ☐ F ☐
Address _____ Apt. No. _____
City _____ State _____ Zip _____
Date of Birth _____ Phone _____
School Name _____ Date of Graduation _____
Academic Major _____
Social Security No. * _____

*This information, voluntarily submitted, will be used for recruiting purposes. Failure to provide sufficient information may preclude action on your inquiry. (Authority 10 U.S.C. 503.)

ATG052

Air Force
A great way of life.

Is This Child Marked For Mental Illness?

You helped build a future for children without the fear of polio, diphtheria and smallpox. Your support of scientific research helped conquer these dread diseases . . . but what of mental illness? Mental illness strikes more children and adults . . . it creates more tragedy and waste of human lives . . . than all other diseases combined. Help science conquer mental illness.

Support Your Local Chapter of the National Association for Mental Health

More non-profit memories: supporting colleges, Air Force recruiting and the National Association for Mental Health.

Chapter 20

ETHICS, CORPORATE SUSTAINABILITY AND GOVERNANCE

I n order to succeed and thrive in modern society, all private and public sector entities must live by codes of ethics. In an era that encompasses mistrust of business, uncertainties about the economy and growing disillusionment within society's structure, it is vital for every organization to determine, analyze, fine-tune and communicate their value systems.

Ethics is more than just a statement that a committee whips together. It is more than a slogan or rehash of a Mission Statement. It is an ongoing dialog that companies have with themselves.

We must understand how to use power and influence for positive change. How we meet corporate objectives is as important as the objectives themselves. Ethics and profits are not conflicting goals. Unethical dealings for short-term gain do not pay off ultimately. Good judgment comes from experience, which, in turn comes from bad judgment. Business must be receptive—not combative—to differing opinions.

Ethics relates to every stage in the evolution of a business, leadership development, mentoring and creative ways of doing business. It is an understanding how and why any organization remains standing and growing, instead of continuing to look at micro-niche parts.

Integrity is personal and professional. It is about more than the contents of a financial report. It bespeaks to every aspect of the way in which we do business. Integrity requires consistency and the enlightened self-interest of doing a better job.

Financial statements by themselves cannot nor ever were intended to determine company value. The enlightened company must be structured, plan and benchmark according to all seven categories on my trademarked Business Tree™: core business, running the business, financial, people, business development, Body of Knowledge (interaction of each part to the other and to the whole) and The Big Picture (who the organization really is, where it is going and how it will successfully get there).

One need not fear business nor think ill of it because of the recent corporate scandals. One need not fear globalization and expansion of business because of economic recessions. It is during the downturns that strong, committed and ethical businesses renew their energies to move forward. The good apples polish their luster in such ways as to distance from the few bad apples.

Mandated reforms cannot take the place of personal responsibility, company ethics programs and industry standards that uphold values. No piece of legislation can cause sweeping actions overnight.

Taking the Ethical High Road, Reading the Signs.

Ethics means operating a business in ways that meet or exceed the ethical, legal, commercial and public expectations that society has of business. This is a comprehensive set of strategies, methodologies, policies, practices and programs that are integrated throughout business operations, supported and rewarded by top management.

The value of corporate responsibility can be measured in quantitative and qualitative ways. Companies have experienced bottom-line benefits, including improved financial performance, reduced operating costs, access to capital, increased sales and customer loyalty, positive reactions to brand image and reputation, heightened productivity, employee commitments to quality, empowered loyal workforces and reduced regulatory oversight.

Corporate Social Responsibility is concerned with treating stakeholders of the company ethically or in a socially responsible manner. Consequently, behaving socially responsibly will increase the human development of stakeholders both within and outside the corporation.

Corporate Sustainability aligns an organization's products and services with stakeholder expectations, thereby adding economic, environmental and social value. This looks at how good companies become better.

Corporate Governance constitutes a balance between economic and social goals and between individual and community goals. The corporate governance framework is there to encourage the efficient use of resources and equally to require accountability for community stewardship of those resources.

Burst Bubbles, Being Refilled

Perception is reality. It is no longer sufficient to pay lip service to ethical issues, such as investor protection, consumer accountability, issues management, protecting the environment and diversity. Concern must be demonstrated. The public needs to see action on every company's part. The same holds true for public sector institutions.

Credibility is formed by the ability to impact all other issues. Total quality means that we must communicate cross-culturally. Find out what people need to know, when they need it and then deliver it.

Organizations who fail to address ethical issues of the day are endangered species. Whatever the public expects of companies, then those companies should expect the same of themselves. My concerns revolve around these areas:

1. Society that Produced the Business Scandals. If we decry the scandals and wrong doing, then modern society must accept our roles in letting them happen.

Too many artificial measurements abound and are based upon flash, sizzle and hucksterism. Having the weekend movie box office grosses for movies on TV and in newspapers every Monday is bogus. Momentary box office grosses are not accurate measures of a film's worth. So much coverage of sales volumes leads media pundits to use ludicrous terms like "X knocked off Y this weekend." When the public hears that misleading statements, they start talking that way too. The public consciousness needs to get away from teasers and slogans.

Anybody who hangs their hats on changeable, temporary rankings is headed for a fall. Top rankings as the ultimate measure of worth and value lead to cottage industries that manipulate the numbers. Bogus research gets purchased. Inflated production reports, unrealistic market shares and improvement quotes receive the spin of those vested in perpetuating the myths. Projecting futures by past momentary successes will escalate the sweepstakes mentality. As long as the media keeps posting movie box office receipts as the only measure of films' standing, then films will be made to match those criteria.

Business has turned into a smoke and mirrors aura. When perceptions matter more than realities and hype more than substance, then the stakes keep escalating to a frenzy. They parlayed the hype to the media, who conveyed to the public, who re-conveyed to each other via idol chatter. The buzz created an unrealistic stock marketed, populated by get-rich-quick day traders.

The frenzy for slogans and clever quips has anointed the word "solutions" into the business lexicon. Solutions are vendor commodities that appeal to purchasers who don't know any better. We keep investing in technology, rather than developing "human intelligence." We buy "solutions" from providers rather than address real, systemic and long-term challenges and opportunities for the company.

The computer consulting industry gave us the Y2K event in 1999, a fever frenzy that was designed to generate billings for consulting, training and sales of technology. American business spent more than $600 billion on Y2K consulting, paying for it by cutting such more important activities as strategic planning, training, employee compensation and marketing. Research shows that 91-99% of those problems never would have occurred. The vendors perpetuated the spin that their work kept the problems from occurring, with unsuspecting buyers believing and perpetuating the justifications.

2. Accounting. Too much emphasis and control of business has been placed in the hands of accountants. Their focus is micro-niche (only about 2% of the Big Picture of business), and to turn over all framing of business issues to accountants is shortsighted. Large accounting firms have influenced the system in their favor. Public companies must be audited by one of them, thus creating as monopoly situation that cuts qualified mid-sized and local accounting firms out of public company work.

Accountants see business through the financial dimension. To pick most the top management from the financial ranks tends to perpetuate the myopic viewpoint. Accounting firms are notorious at not wanting to collaborate with other consultants and professional disciplines. By not allowing other perspectives on their radars and controlling the business model in their favor, a continuum of sameness has occurred. It will continue to occur until business widens its scope and perspective.

3. CEOs. Too much romanticism has been placed upon the term CEO by others who want to be rewarded by them. No Chief Executive Officer by himself or herself can make or break a company. They need codependents in order to do damage. The company that lays down all the gold to one CEO in hopes of magical results is inviting being ripped off.

Conversely, as a reaction to corporate scandals the term CEO is currently in disfavor. The public decries CEOs for the same reasons that we canonize them. People envy the power, status and wealth and cannot fathom the endless behind-the-scenes work conducted by reputable CEOs and management teams.

Most CEOs are not adequately groomed for their roles as company role model and leader. They come from the ranks of core business or financial, without proper exposure to other facets that make a winning company. Thus, they surround themselves with like minds or yes-men. Many CEOs do not take counsel of qualified experts, thus remaining isolated, partially-focused and lonely at the top.

A CEO is only as good as the team that he-she leads. A top CEO fulfills roles and responsibilities across every business unit. The CEO must amass people skills, marketing savvy, planning expertise, quality orientation, leadership tenets, marketplace championing and much more. The days of the internal, bottom-line-only-focused CEO are long obsolete.

4. Boards of Directors. Companies must hold boards of directors, management teams, mid-manager ranks and line directors more accountable. These folks expect financial rewards and must be more accountable. They must work in collaboration with the CEO, not as pawns of his-her ideology. Chapter 13 covered the dynamics of board service and the myriad of responsibilities that good directors undertake.

Widening the Frame of Business Reference

Ethics is the science of morals, rightness and obligations in human affairs. Institutions must conduct many activities which impact their general welfare. Ethical issues go beyond nice rhetoric and must encompass duties, principles, values, processes, responsibilities and governing methodologies.

Organizations who fail to address ethical issues of the day are endangered species. Whatever the public expects of companies, then those companies should expect the same of themselves.

The Ethics Statement must be more than a terse branding slogan. Like the Mission Statement in the Strategic Plan, it is the amalgamation of careful thought, weighed insights and tests for fairness and durability. The Ethics Statement must be a part of the Strategic Plan, as are such other fundamental statements covering customer-focused management, diversity, valuing stakeholders, quality management and an empowered workforce.

Every organization differs in how it will implement Corporate Responsibility and Ethics programs. The differences are factored by the company's size, sector, culture and the commitment of its leadership. Some companies focus on a single area of operation. The Code of Ethics may include Fundamental Canons, Rules of Practice and Professional Obligations.

Business ethics encompass much more than accounting fraud and the publicly stated values of stocks. Ethics should be attached to many other important areas of business. Elements in the Ethics internal company review, which could subsequently be addressed in the full ethics plan, may include:

- Accountability by all top managers.
- Accountability by all mid-managers.
- Accountability by all board members.
- Fair practices regarding collaborators, suppliers and vendors.
- Codes of conduct, standards and guidelines.
- Security issues.
- Financial reporting, accounting and disclosures.
- Statement of assets.
- Professional development, training and education goals.
- Performance reviews.
- Workplace issues.
- Diversity.
- Benchmarks of progress.
- Marketplace activities, competition and intelligence.
- Community investment.
- The environment.
- Strategic management.
- Strategic planning.
- Corporate citizenship.
- Accounting principles.
- Auditing standards.
- Compilation and review standards.
- Technical standards.
- Reputation assurance.
- Social accountability.
- Compliance with all applicable laws (to the letter and spirit).
- Meet and exceed guidelines of regulators.
- Protection of purchasers of equipment and systems.
- Reliable treatment of vendors, suppliers and partners.
- Treat as confidential all information learned about the business of a customer.
- Full disclosures.

- Responsible advertising, promotions and public statements about the company.
- Reliable representations about products and services.
- Accurate representation of experience and capabilities of employees and agents.
- Integrity, objectivity and independence.

The corporate ethics program may include a code of ethics, training for employees for ethical behaviors, a means for communicating with employees, reporting mechanism, audit system, investigation system, compliance strategy, prevention strategy and integrity strategy. The program seeks to create conditions that support the right actions. It communicates the values and vision of the organization. It aligns the standards of employees with those of the organization and relies upon the entire management team, not just the legal and compliance personnel.

A formal and well documented corporate ethics program will prevent ethical misconduct, monetary losses and losses to reputation. If communicated well, it may breed customer trust. In fact, I highly recommend using executive summaries of the ethics program as a corporate communications tool. The sending of the Ethics Statement to customers, suppliers, regulators and other stakeholders demonstrates the extra length to which the company goes to become a model. It becomes a good marketing mailing, and it's the right thing to do.

As part of strategic planning, corporate ethics helps the organization to adapt to rapid change, regulatory changes, mergers and global competition. It helps to manage relations with stakeholders. It enlightens partners and suppliers about a company's own standards. It reassures other stakeholders as to the company's intent.

Chapter 21

LEADERSHIP PROGRAMS

Leadership for Organizations Developing the Right Talent to Reach the Next Level

I
t's lonely at the top. Executives must develop themselves for the next level and to be useful to their companies and communities in the future. This chapter is a primer for executives and the heirs apparent to company leadership. Critical topics include leadership development of executives, mindset changes in the evolution from manager to executive to leader, executive mentoring, insights into how top professionals evolve, plateaus of professional accomplishment, developing a winning work ethic, lifelong learning and the accrual of business wisdom.

Not all executives are leaders. Not all managers are executives. Not all career people are professional. A major problem with organizations stems from the fact that management and company leadership come from one small piece of the organizational pie. Filling all management slots with financial people, for example, serves to limit the organizational strategy and focus. They all hire like-minded people and frame every business decision from their micro perspective.

The ideal executive has strong leadership skills first. He or she develops organizational vision and sets strategies. Leaders should reflect a diversity of focus, guaranteeing that a balance is achieved. The best management team looks at the macro, rather than just the niche micro.

None of us was born with sophisticated, finely tuned senses and highly enlightened viewpoints for life. We muddle through, try our best and get hit in the gut several times. Thus, we learn, amass knowledge and turn most experiences into strategies. Such a perspective is what makes seasoned executives valuable in the business marketplace.

Life has a way of forcing the human condition to change. Events which may inspire this to happen could include a recognition that the old methods are not working, financial failures or the monetary incentive to rapidly create or change plans of action. At most crossroads, there is no choice but to change the modus operandi. This may include the loss of substantial numbers of opportunities, customers, employees and market share or a "wake up call" of any type.

There are six generations in the population. Generations, the accurate definitions: Greatest Generation, persons born through 1926. Silent Generation, persons born 1927-1945. Baby Boomers, persons born 1946-1964. Generation X, persons born 1965-1983. Generation Y, Millennials, persons born 1984-2002. Generation Z, persons born 2003-2021. These are the correct figures (wrong ranges elsewhere on the internet).

The most effective leaders accept that change is 90% positive and find reasons and rationale to embrace change. Leadership skills are learned and synthesized daily. Knowledge is usually amassed through unexpected sources.

Management Styles

In the period that predated scientific management, the Captain of Industry style prevailed. Prior to 1885, the kings of industry were rulers, as had been land barons of earlier years. Policies were dictated, and people complied. Some captains were notoriously ruthless. Others like Rockefeller, Carnegie and Ford channeled their wealth and power into giving back to the communities. It was an era of self-made millionaires and the people who toiled in their mills.

From 1885-1910, the labor movement gathered steam. Negotiations and collective bargaining focused on conditions for workers and physical plant environments. In this era, business fully segued from an agricultural-based economy to an industrial-based reality.

As a counterbalance for industrial reforms and the strength of unions, a Hard Nosed style of leadership was prominent from 1910-1939. This was management's attempt to take stronger hands, recapture some of the Captain of Industry style and build solidity into an economy plagued by the Depression. This is an important phase to remember because it is the mindset of addictive organizations.

The Human Relations style of management flourished from 1940-1964. Under it, people were managed. Processes were managed as collections of people. Employees began having greater says in the execution of policies. Yet, the rank and file employees at this point were not involved in creating policies, least of all strategies and methodologies.

Management by Objectives came into vogue in 1965 and was the prevailing leadership style until 1990. In this era, business started embracing formal planning. Other important components of business (training, marketing, research, team building and productivity) were all accomplished according to goals, objectives and tactics.

In 1991, Customer Focused Management became the standard. It will be discussed at length in this chapter.

Most corporate leaders are two management styles behind. Those who matured in the era of the Human Relations style of management were still clinging to value systems of Hard Nosed. They were not just "old school." They went to the school that was torn down to build the old school.

Executives who were educated in the Management by Objectives era were still recalling value systems of their parents' generation before it. Baby boomers with a Depression-era frugality and value of tight resources are more likely to take a bean counter-focused approach to business. That's my concern that financial-only focus without regard to other corporate dynamics bespeaks of hostile takeovers, ill-advised rollups and corporate raider activity in search of acquiring existing books of business.

To follow through the premise, younger executives who were educated and came of age during the early years of Customer Focused Management had still not comprehended and embraced its tenets. As a result, the dot.com bust and subsequent financial scandals occurred. In a nutshell, the "new school" of managers did not think that corporate protocols and strategies related to them. The game was to just write the rules as they rolled along. Such thinking always invites disaster, as so many of their stockholders found out. Given that various management eras are still reflected in the new order of business, we must learn from each and move forward.

Leadership for the New Order

Within every corporate and structure, there exists a stair-step ladder. One enters the ladder at some professional level and is considered valuable for the category of services for which he or she has expertise. This ladder holds true for managers and employees within the organization, as well as outside consultants brought in.

Each professional rung on the ladder is important. At whatever level one enters the ladder, he-she should be trained, measured for performance and fit into the organization's overall scope. These are the stages of leadership:

1. Resource. One has experience with equipment, tools, materials and schedules.
2. Skills and Tasks. One is concerned with activities, procedures and project fulfillment.
3. Role and Job. The position is defined according to assignments, responsibilities, functions, relationships, follow-through and accountability.
4. Systems and Processes. These are managers, concerned with structure, hiring, control, work design, supervision and the effects of management decisions.
5. Strategy. These executives spend much of their energies on planning, tactics, organizational development and business development.

6. Culture and Mission. Upper management is most effective when it frames business decisions toward values, customs, beliefs, goals, objectives and the benchmarking of tactics.

7. Philosophy. These are the visionaries who advise management in refining the organizational purpose, vision, quality of life, ethics and contributions toward the company's long-term growth.

One rarely advances more than one rung on the ladder during the course of service to the organization unless he-she embodies that wider scope. The professional who succeeds the most is the one who sees himself-herself in the bigger picture and contextualizes what they do accordingly.

Value-added leadership is a healthy way of professional life that puts collaborations first. When all succeed, then profitability is much higher and more sustained than under the Hard Nose management style.

Value-added leadership requires a senior team commitment. Managers and employees begin seeing themselves as leaders and grow steadily into those roles. It is not acceptable to be a clone of what you perceive someone else to be. Those organizations and managers who use terms like "world class" are usually wanna-be's who won't ever quite make the measuring stick.

Leadership means being consistently excellent and upholding standards to remain so. There is no such thing as perfection. Yet, excellence is a definitive process of achievement, dedication and expeditious use of resources. Exponential improvement each year is the objective.

Good professionals must be role models. Leadership comes from inner quests, ethical pursuits and professional diligence. Often, we teach others what we were never taught or what we learned the hard way. That's how this book came into being…there was no executive encyclopedia for those to make it long-term. Those who take that knowledge into practice will lead their business and industry.

If every executive devoted at least 10% of his-her time to these activities, then corporate scandals would not occur. Thinking and reasoning skills are not taught in school, and they are amassed through a wealth of professional experiences. Planning is the thread woven through this book, and it is the key to the future. One can never review progress enough, with benchmarking being the key to implementing plans.

Many organizations fall into the trap of calling what they are doing a "tradition." That is an excuse used by many to avoid change and accountability. Just because something has been done one or two times, realize that it will get old and stale. Traditions are philosophies that are regularly fine-tuned, with elements added. Traditions are not stuck in ruts, though failing companies are.

If I could determine curriculum, every business school would require public speaking and writing courses. I'd have every professional development program devote more to leadership and thinking skills than they do to computer training. I'd also have courses with such titles as "The Business Executive as Community Leader," "Mentoring Your Own Staff" and "Role Model 101."

Management Leads in Great Organizations

Companies that are planned and have developed strategies to meet the future now subscribe to results based management, with the goal to improve program effectiveness, accountability and achieve results. This means that company leadership is committed to:

- Establishing clear organizational vision, mission and priorities, which are translated into a four-year framework of goals, outputs, indicators, strategies and resources.
- Encouraging an organizational and management culture that promotes innovation, learning, accountability, and transparency.
- Delegating authority, empowering managers and holding them accountable for results.
- Focusing on achieving results, through strategic planning, regular monitoring of progress, evaluation of performance, and reporting on performance.
- Creating supportive mechanisms, policies and procedures, building and improving on what is already in place.
- Sharing information, knowledge, learning lessons and feeding these back into improving decision-making and performance.

- Optimizing human resources and building capacity among staff to manage for results.
- Making the best use of financial resources in an efficient manner to achieve results.
- Strengthening and diversifying partnerships at all levels.
- Responding to external situations and needs within the organizational mandate.

We are the products of those who believe in us. Find role models and set out to be one yourself. To get, you must give. Career and life are not a short stint. Do what it takes to run the decathlon. Set personal and professional goals, standards and accountability.

Stand for something. Making money is not enough. You must do something worth leaving behind, mentoring to others and of recognizable substance. Your views of professionalism must be known and shown.

Mentorship and Lifelong Learning

Professionals who succeed the most are the products of mentoring. I heartily endorse that find a great mentor. I have had many excellent ones in my long career and have in turn mentored hundreds of others.

The mentor is a resource for business trends, societal issues and opportunities. The mentor becomes a role model, offering insights about their own life-career. This reflection shows the mentee levels of thinking and perception which were not previously available. The mentor is an advocate for progress and change. Such work empowers the mentee to hear, accept, believe and get results. The sharing of trust and ideas leads to developing business philosophies.

The mentor endorses the mentee, messages ways to approach issues, helps draw distinctions and paints pictures of success. The mentor opens doors for the mentee. The mentor requests pro-active changes of mentee, evaluates realism of goals and offers truths about path to success and shortcomings of mentee's approaches. This is a bonded collaboration toward each other's success. The mentor stands for mentees throughout their careers and celebrates their successes. This is a lifelong dedication toward mentorship…in all aspects of one's life.

The most significant lessons that I learned in my business life from mentors, verified with experience, are shared here:

1. You cannot go through life as a carbon copy of someone else.
2. You must establish your own identity, which is a long, exacting process.
3. As you establish a unique identity, others will criticize. Being different, you become a moving target.
4. People criticize you because of what you represent, not who you are. It is rarely personal against you. Your success may bring out insecurities within others. You might be what they cannot or are not willing to become.
5. If you cannot take the dirtiest job in any company and do it yourself, then you will never become "management."
6. Approach your career as a body of work. This requires planning, purpose and commitment. It's a career, not just a series of jobs.
7. The person who is only identified with one career accomplishment or by the identity of one company for whom he-she formerly worked is a one-hit wonder and, thus, has no body of work.
8. The management that takes steps to "fix themselves" rather than always projecting problems upon other people will have a successful organization.
9. It's not when you learn. It's that you learn.
10. Many people do without the substantive insights into business because they have not really developed critical thinking skills.
11. Analytical and reasoning skills are extensions of critical thinking skills.
12. You perform your best work for free. How you fulfill commitments and pro-bono work speaks to the kind of professional that you are.
13. People worry so much what others think about them. If they knew how little others thought, they wouldn't worry so much. This too is your challenge to frame how they see you and your company.
14. Fame is fleeting and artificial. The public is fickle and quick to jump on the newest flavor, without showing loyalty to the old ones, especially

those who are truly original. Working in radio, I was taught, "They only care about you when you're behind the microphone."

15. The pioneer and "one of a kind" professional has a tough lot in life. It is tough to be first or so far ahead of the curve that others cannot see it. Few will understand you. Others will attain success with portions of what you did. None will do it as well.

16. Consumers are under-educated and don't know the substance of a pioneer. Our society takes more to the copycats and latest fads. Only the pioneer knows and appreciates what he-she really accomplished. That reassurance will have to be enough.

17. Life and careers include peaks and valleys. It's how one copes during the "down times" that is the true measure of success.

18. Long-term success must be earned. It is not automatic and is worthless if ill-gotten. The more dues one pays, the more you must continue paying.

19. The next best achievement is the one you're working on now, inspired by your body of knowledge to date.

20. The person who never has aggressively pursued a dream or mounted a series of achievements cannot understand the quest of one with a deeply committed dream.

21. A great percentage of the population does not achieve huge goals but still admires and learns from those who do persevere and succeed. The achiever thus becomes a lifelong mentor to others.

22. Achievement is a continuum, but it must be benchmarked and enjoyed along the way.

These are my concluding pieces of leadership advice. Know where you are going. Develop, update and maintain a career growth document. Keep a diary of lessons learned but not soon forgotten. Learn the reasons for success and, more importantly, from failure.

Good bosses were good employees. They have keen understanding for both roles. Bad bosses likely were not ideal employees. They too are consistent in career history.

Being your own boss is yet another lesson. People who were downsized from a corporate environment suddenly enter the entrepreneurial world and find the transition to be tough.

Poor people skills cloud any job performance and overshadow good technical skills. The worst bosses do not sustain long careers at the top. Their track record catches up with them, whether they choose to acknowledge it or not.

Good workers don't automatically become good bosses. Just because someone is technically proficient or is an exemplary producer does not mean that he-she will transition to being a boss. The best school teachers do not want to become principals, for that reason. Good job performers are better left doing what they do best. Administrators, at all levels, need to be properly trained as such, not bumped up from the field to do something for which they have no inclination.

Truth and ethics must be woven into how you conduct business. If you do not "walk the talk," who will? Realize that very little of what happens to you in business is personal. Find common meeting grounds with colleagues. The only workable solution is a win-win.

Leadership and executive development skills are steadily learned and continually sharpened. One course or a quick-read book will not instill them. The best leaders are prepared to go the distance. Professional enrichment must be life-long. Early formal education is but a starting point. Study trends in business, in your industry and in the industries of your customers.

People skills mastery applies to every profession. There is no organization that does not have to communicate to others about what it does. The process of open company dialogs must be developed to address conflicts, facilitate win-win solutions and further organizational goals.

Chapter 22

AWARDS AND RECOGNITION

Take a Look, Improve, Everyone Benefits

This chapter centers upon an area that encompasses both leadership and teamwork skills. This is an area of business where few top executives were ever mentored. This is a primer on recognition, the attention they bring and the ultimate benefits of continuous improvement, plus the inspiration to keep doing an excellent job.

Awards and recognition are very important for businesses. Everyone likes to be associated with a winner. If certain kinds of companies have not received awards, one might rightfully suspect why. Such is the status of modern society.

There are some companies whose quest for recognition goes to extremes. However, those who do good work should indeed be recognized publicly for it. Tooting one's horn is a reflection of excellent work, and one need not be embarrassed by external recognition. Awards become a marketing tool and, more importantly, become the call to keep besting one's company in the eyes of customers, employees and stakeholders.

I have won more than 150 awards in my long career. Most were for client projects in juried competitions. Many were for civic leadership and service to non-profit causes. A few were awarded by virtue of staying power in a variety of business and community arenas. In addition to that were the certificates, children's artwork, photos and other memorabilia presented as thanks for acts of kindness, garnered from decades of doing things which I just saw as being a good citizen.

In some cultures, the notion of achieving notoriety, winning awards, championing civic causes and attaining notoriety for your company is unheard of. A few years ago, I was asked by the Japanese-American Chamber of Commerce to write a handbook on giving back to the community and why it is important in the Western world. This is contrary to the low-profile stance that business leaders take in Asia, Latin America and the Middle East.

While speaking and consulting businesses in Kuwait, I was asked to present a program on the Western world non-profit culture and why business must get involved with causes. Often in work in Latin America and Europe, questions about the value of cause-related marketing came up from interested parties wishing to participate but wondering how far to go in attracting attention to themselves.

When you win enough awards in your career, one gets asked to judge other programs. In my case, those included programs for the Malcolm Baldridge Quality Award, United Way of America, National Association for Community Leadership, Associated General Contractors, American Education Association, Harvard Business School and others. Each time, I was honored to volunteer time and serve. Each time, I learned much and was inspired by those honorable, sincere companies who applied. As a judge, you want everyone to do well, and you believe all of them to be winners.

Through my membership in a think tank called the Silver Fox Advisors, I joined my friends in judging as Better Business Bureau awards program. As one who works with the world's largest corporations, I was there reading application forms from movers, janitorial service companies, mechanics, plumbers, technology providers and the entire rainbow of local small business.

You could tell that company owners were stretching beyond their comfort zones to answer all the questions. These were low-key people who just worked hard and served their customers well. Now, the entrants had to write their business philosophies for outsiders to review. While these narratives may not reflect the weighty language that I use in this book, they indeed reflected a group of sincere company owners who were trying to do their very best. Their answers to questions about ethical dilemmas and putting customer crises first were the kinds of comments that bureaucracy-ridden corporations would never be caught rendering. I wondered why cannot all businesses be as honorable and responsive as those small business owners who entered that program.

Subsequently, a fellow awards judge and I appeared on a radio show to promote the awards winners. The CEO of one of the winning companies said that the application made him think long and hard about his business, being totally honest about many facets and uncovering needs for improvement in other areas. Bravo for his insights. I stated that awards applications should be thought of as executive summaries for company strategic plans. These analyses should then become the lynchpin for the next visioning process and how the organization will vault top the next tier.

One year, I had received several awards. I got a Savvy Award, for the top three community leaders. I was a Dewar's profile subject. I had gotten a standing ovation at the United Nations for volunteer work that was my honor to do (especially since it enabled me to work with my favorite actress, Audrey Hepburn).

Subsequently, I was participating in a community stewardship awards judging. I quizzed, "Why is it that the same old names keep popping up? There are great people to honor other that those of us from business, high society or other top-of-the-mind awareness. What this community needs is an awards program that people like us cannot win."

I was then challenged to come up with such a program, the result being the Leadership in Action Awards for the City of Houston. I wrote a four-page application that was long and detailed, asking some very tough questions. To enter this program, non-profit organizations per each category (arts, education, health causes, diversity, etc.) had to enter as teams, not as individuals. They had to justify donations, volunteer usage, partnerships, in-kind services, public sector support and other criteria. Then, they had to answer accountability and program evaluation questions.

We staged a seminar for prospective entrants and gave pointers on filling out the complete application, to help avoid the stock material that some might otherwise submit. Those who attended the application preparation seminar did indeed fare better in the judging process. At the judging, we were all impressed with how well these "unsung heroes" in the community described their non-profit programs.

At the awards presentation banquet, the swell of pride from the winning organizations, their directors, their volunteers and even some of their clients was heartening to see. These unsung heroes were finally getting their just recognition for community work well done. The corporate donors who supported them had every right to be proud.

At the following year's awards preparation seminar, last year's winners also spoke. One said that this was the toughest application they had ever filled out. They had since submitted material contained in our application to foundations and got more funding than expected because they volunteered so much more information than had been required. Because their awards were based upon genuine team efforts, these programs received much more support from their boards, funding sources and constituencies.

I believe that every business must go after some forms of recognition because the process offers levels of objective judgment and criticism necessary to sustain the business. One cannot go after awards just for glorification reasons. However, recognition programs are a balanced scorecard that involves the scrutiny of the company and its leaders by credible outside sources.

Awards inspire companies of all sizes to work harder and try more creative things. Good deeds in the community are not done for the awards; they just represent good business. Receiving recognition after the fact for works that were attempted for right and noble reasons is the icing on the cake that employees need. Good people aspire to higher goals. Every business leader needs to be groomed as a community leader.

Recognition for a track record of contributions represents more than "tooting one's own horn." It is indicative of the kind of organizations with whom you are honored to do business. The more that one is recognized and honored, the harder that one works to keep the luster and its integrity shiny.

Every community should sponsor a business awards recognition program. If the municipality does not have one, it should start such a program. Potential co-sponsors could include newspapers, Better Business Bureau chapters, business schools, chambers of commerce, Rotary and other service clubs, professional associations and non-profit community leadership organizations.

The process of entering juried awards competition should be seen as the next step toward company visioning. The narrative becomes an executive summary for the next strategic plan. Awards for which someone else nominates you are meritorious honors, reflecting your body of work and well-earned reputation.

Being the recipient of awards gives you the opportunity to market your company in a tasteful manner. Always reframe the recognition back to the customers, as a recommitment toward serving them better and further.

Chapter 23

THE QUALITY PROCESS IS A MINDSET THAT POISES ORGANIZATIONS FOR SUCCESS

Quality is not something that managers assign others to achieve. It is a mindset that permeates organizations from top-down as well as bottom-up. Rather than assume all is wrong or right with an organization and take a defensive posture, management must view quality as essential to their economic survival or growth.

Quality entails four concepts:

1. Success is determined by conformity to requirements.
2. It is achieved through prevention, not appraisal. The quality audit by objective outside communications counsel is merely the beginning of a process.
3. The quality performance standard is zero defects. That means doing things correctly the first time, without wasting counter-productive time in cleaning up mistakes.
4. Nonconformance is costly. Make-good efforts cost more on the back end than doing things right on the front end.

Organizations measure quality by overall involvement. It is not enough for management to endorse quality programs; they must actively participate.

Quality should be viewed as a journey, rather than a destination. It applies to service industries and manufacturing operations. Even non-profit and public sector organizations must utilize quality approaches for staff and volunteer councils/boards.

Employees must buy into the process by offering constructive input. All ideas are worthy of consideration. Life-threatening experiences (loss of business or market share, economic recession) signal the urgency for the team to collaborate.

Empowerment of employees means they accept the challenges and consequences. They must view the company as a consumer would, being as discerning about buying their own services as they are about fine dining, premium clothing, gifts for friends, a car or a home.

What if we were all paid based upon customer perceptions of our service? That would make each of us more attentive to what we offer and whether our value is correctly perceived.

Each member of an organization must view himself/herself as having customers. Each must be seen as a profit center and as having something valuable to contribute to the overall group. Each is a link that lets down the whole chain by failing to uphold their part.

What is missing in most organizations is the willingness to move forward, not the availability of information or desire for improvement. Willingness requires complete and never-ending commitment by management. The first time the organization tolerates anything less than 100%, it is on the road back to mediocrity.

The most common pitfalls toward success include:

- Taking a piecemeal approach to quality.
- Thinking that quality needs apply to some other department, company or industry, not your own.
- Thinking that you are already doing things "the quality way."
- Failing to address structural flaws that fuel the problems.

- Focusing upon esoteric techniques, rather than true reasons for instilling quality.
- Saying that something is being done when it is not.
- Failing to engage customers and suppliers into the process.
- Failing to emphasize training.
- Setting goals that are too low.
- Communicating poorly with the organization and its publics. Without employee communications, suggestion boxes, publications, training videos, speeches and other professionally prepared instruments, the company is fooling itself and its customers about the commitment to quality. Without good communication from the outset, the program will never be understood and accepted.

Quality improvement is the only action that can simultaneously win the support of customers, employees, investors, media and the public. Productivity translates to profitability in an advantageous climate in which to function.

The Quality Process Is an Investment Toward Economic Survival and Growth

Research shows the by-product costs of poor quality are high for any business, up to 40 percent. Lack of attentiveness to quality has cost the United States its global marketplace dominance. Other nations preceded the U.S. in adopting the quality process and overtook our nation in many areas.

Success via competitiveness has many dimensions. Production efficiency became America's focus by the 1950s.

Marketing's importance was fully embraced in the 1960s. Marketing departments deal most often and immediately with the side effects of poor quality.

The 1970s brought the first wave of strategic planning. Without mapping a course, how can any organization reach a destination?

The 1980s brought us the quality process, which is the bow that wraps a package containing the other three elements. At the start of the decade, many executives viewed the quality process with indifference or fear. By decade's end, virtually all (92%) agreed that quality was the main prescription for survival.

Though quality is one element of competitiveness, it cannot cover defects in the other areas. The quality audit by objective outside communications counsel can also examine the production, marketing and strategic planning functions.

Companies must place demands upon their own organizations to embrace customer service tenets. Satisfied customers talk to others, encouraging them to buy based upon quality of the company. Dissatisfied customers will aggressively discourage higher numbers of prospects from buying.

The mark of any professional is the manner in which he/she corrects mistakes. Most often, this means correcting misperceptions about company attitude, rather than the condition of goods. The faster the correction, the better the level of satisfaction. Quality is the sum of impressions made on the customer.

Payroll is the biggest overhead item. Improvement can be quantified by increased productivity, reduced turnover and heightened employee morale.

The empowered team is trusted to seek quality on their own. Bad managers will fall by the wayside. Employees who do not pull their share will stick out like sore thumbs. The team will not be judged by the superstars but, instead, by the average. The whole is greater than the sum of its parts.

In order to complete the chain, organizations must insist that suppliers, professional services counselors and vendors show demonstrated quality programs, as well as ethics statements. Educational and incentive programs should be implemented. During tough economic times, investment in a quality program is not costly. Anyone who is unwilling to spend for quality is hastening company decline.

Strategy Steers the Quality Process

Quality is one of the most vital ingredients of competitive success. Total Quality Management (TQM) is recognized as a prerequisite for survival. One fourth of all corporations now administer quality programs.

The focus on quality has gone beyond the finished product and addresses all processes throughout the organization. Evaluating quality is not just a question of meeting customers' expectations, but rather exceeding them.

Paying attention to quality can realize:

- Lower operating costs. Research shows they can be cut in half.
- Premium pricing for preferred goods/services.
- Customer retention.
- Enhanced reputation.
- Access to global markets.
- Faster innovation.
- Higher sales.
- Higher return on investments. TQM has increased profitability in some corporations up to six times.

Total Quality Management is customer-focused and strategy-directed. It is a top management activity, steered by public relations counselors. The human relations component is strong, but quality programs are substantially communications-driven.

The successful quality program empowers employees, who will achieve quality on their own. The more positive results are shown, the more universal will be participation.

The quality process must have substance—not just rhetoric—in order to build momentum. There are no magic shortcuts. If the process is given proper attention and support by top management, it is a money-maker.

How to Institute a Quality Program

Change is painful for most people but is necessary. Conducting "business as usual" means standing still, which means losing ground while other companies move forward.

Quality does not mean that true perfection will exist. It is simply a commitment to keep the wheels of progress at top-of-mind motion.

To change and improve requires methodically and systematically undertaking actions that will make your company "world class." These actions include:

- Education.
- Communication.
- Reward and recognition.
- Employee suggestion systems.
- Involvement teams.
- Benchmark measurements of accomplishments.
- Statistical management methods.

Most companies implement quality programs as a reaction to a perceived negative image. Data is gathered in scattered areas, usually to produce flashy charts for customers. Because upper management does not know which programs to implement, the quality process stagnates.

Doing things for the wrong reasons or to temporarily pacify someone else spells failure. There are no quick fixes. Applying short-term approaches will just reopen the wounds at a later date. Quality can never be identified too broadly enough.

In order to put a quality program into place, the following steps must be taken:

- Study the activities of admired companies. Interview them to provide insight. Set meetings to review what works for them. Read case studies of Malcolm Baldridge Award winners. Companies can and should be role models for each other.
- Retain outside experts. Quality programs are communications driven and should be captained by public relations counsel who possess this expertise. They will conduct communications audits and strategic planning. This is not something that can be conducted alone by internal human resources departments. Good experts will tell you the hard facts and what needs to be done.

- Research drives most communications programs. Commission customer and employee surveys. It will provide comparisons between the realities and perceptions that are held.
- Ask counsel to write a plan of action for putting the quality program into place.
- Assemble an internal quality team…making sure that all major departments are represented. Together with outside counsel, this committee will pursue its objectives, per the written agenda.
- Set realistic timelines for putting recommendations into place.
- Set schedules for routine review of the process. This includes repeating surveys to assure that you are making adequate progress.

By successfully combining employee involvement, process improvement, customer focus and demonstrated management endorsement, any company can succeed at quality. Even on a limited investment, quality can be attained.

The challenge is to discover what mix of price and quality the customer wants and to deliver it. Slogans only create adversarial relationships. Once the system owns up to its shortcomings and responsibilities, then a true quality process will occur.

Failure to read the "handwriting on the wall" will thwart company growth and, thus, the overall economy.

Chapter 24

QUIZ ABOUT NON-PROFITS

Who founded the Red Cross?

The American Red Cross began during the Civil War, when Clara Barton took care of wounded soldiers. She recognized the need for medical nursing, supplies at the battlefronts and the need for morale boosts. The international Red Cross organization started in 1863 and encouraged Ms. Barton to create the American chapter. In 1881, she obtained formal recognition and served as its president until 1904. The organization's activities extended to floods, famines, fires and other disasters.

Where were the first CARE Packages sent?

CARE was founded 1945 as the Cooperative for Assistance and Relief Everywhere. It is a non-partisan non-government agency. Packages had been prepared for an invasion of Japan that never transpired. They were diverted by sending CARE packages to countries in Europe that were torn by war. CARE expanded the globe, assisting areas in need with food, supplies and diplomatic service. CARE has helped construct schools and provided philanthropic services across the globe.

Where were the Boy Scouts founded?

Boy Scouts was founded in 1907 in England by Robert Baden Powell. The American scouting program was founded in 1910. Its purpose was to "teach patriotism, courage, self-reliance and kindred values." Learning for Life is a school and work-site subsidiary program of BSA.

When was the first sale of Girl Scout cookies?

Girl Scouts was founded in 1912 by Juliette Gordon Low. That first chapter in Savannah, Georgia, has grown to 3.6 million members throughout the U.S. In 1917, a troop in Oklahoma began baking shortbread cookies in a mother's kitchen and sold the cookies at their local high school. In 1922, Girl Scouts of the USA recommended cookie sales, and a chapter in Philadelphia organized the first drive. Since then, each council has operated its own sales of cookies each year to raise funds in support of programs.

Who has been requested to appear most often by kids in the Make a Wish program?

Make a Wish Foundation was founded in 1980 in Phoenix, Arizona. It arranges experiences for children aged 3-17 with life-threatening conditions, referred by physicians. Wishes are granted through 61 chapters. Professional wrestler John Cena holds the record for the most wishes granted (450), followed by singer Justin Bieber and the National Women's Collegiate Fraternity Chi Omega.

What were the first distance learning education and university courses?

In 1728, the first correspondence course ran an ad in the Boston Gazette. In 1873, the first correspondence schools were offered by The Society to Encourage Studies at Home. In 1892, the University of Chicago was the first traditional educational institution in the U.S. to offer correspondence courses. In 1906, primary schools followed suit. In 1922, radio broadcasting became a viable means of transmitting information, and Pennsylvania State College began broadcasting courses over the radio. In 1925, State University of Iowa began offering course credit for radio broadcast courses. In 1953, KUHT-TV, the first educational TV station in the United States, offered televised college classes for credit. In 1965, the University of Wisconsin began a statewide educational program for physicians in a telephone-based format. In 1976, the first "virtual college" with no physical campus was in operation, Coastline Community College, offering tele-courses.

How did blood banks come into being?

John Braxton Hicks first experimented with chemical methods of preventing coagulation of blood in the 1890s. The first transfusion was performed by Dr. Albert Hustin and Dr. Luis Agote in 1914. The British Red Cross established the first blood donor service in 1921. One of the first blood banks was founded in Barcelona, Spain, in 1936. Dr. Bernard Fanfus began the first hospital blood bank in Chicago, IL, in 1937. The Blood for Britain campaign in 1940 took collections in the U.S. and provided them to the U.K. The plastic bag for blood collection was introduced in 1950. Collection and distribution programs now exist in every community around the world.

Who founded the March of Dimes?

The March of Dimes Foundation was launched in 1938 by President Franklin D. Roosevelt to combat polio. It works to improve the health of mothers and babies.

Which former U.S. President dedicated the rest of his life to humanitarian service?

James Earl Carter was President of the U.S. from 1977-1981, the only U.S. president who once lived in public assistance housing. He was a peanut farmer and Governor of Georgia prior to becoming President. In 1982, he established the Carter Center as the basis for advancing human rights. He has conducted peace negotiations, has monitored 96 elections in 38 nations and has fostered programs to reduce disease in under-developed nations. He has been a major proponent of

Habitat For Humanity. In 2002, he received the Nobel Peace Prize for his work "to find peaceful solutions to international conflicts, to advance democracy and human rights, and to promote economic and social development."

Why did Danny Thomas found St. Jude's Hospital?

When he was a struggling comedian, Danny Thomas vowed to give back future riches to the greater good, praying to his patron saint, St. Jude Thaddeus. St. Jude Children's Research Hospital, a pediatric treatment and research center, was founded in Memphis, TN, in 1962 by entertainer Danny Thomas, with help from Lemuel Diggs and Anthony Abraham. It is non-denominational and open to all. The institution has advanced successes in cancer treatment, pediatric brain tumor treatment and survival from lymphoblastic leukemia. Danny's daughter Marlo is the national spokesperson for St. Jude's, which opened the Marlo Thomas Center for Global Education and Collaboration in 2014.

Why was Bob Geldof knighted?

Bob Geldof is a rock star, leader of the group The Boomtown Rats. He was the driving force behind "Band Aid" in 1984. It was a record featuring the talents of most major British rock stars, to raise funds to assist famine relief in Ethiopia. The song was titled "Do They Know It's Christmas?" Geldof was one of the organizers of the Live Aid concert, a 16-hour extravaganza to raise money and awareness for Africa. He became involved in the work of non-governmental organizations and was the leading spokesperson on Third World debt and relief.

What drew Ronald Reagan into the public arena?

After a long career as a film actor, Ronald Reagan hosted "General Electric Theatre" on CBS-TV from 1952-1962. His duties as ambassador for General Electric Corporation, coupled with his presidency of the Screen Actors Guild inspired him into public service and politics. Ronald Reagan was elected Governor of California in 1966 and President of the United States in 1980.

Who took us into the jungle to better understand the human condition by observing animal lifestyles and behaviors?

Jane Goodall is a humanitarian and environmentalist who has devoted years to studying behaviors of chimpanzees in their native habitat. Observed Ms. Goodall, ""Chimpanzees have given me so much. The long hours spent with them in the forest have enriched my life beyond measure. What I have learned from them has shaped my understanding of human behavior, of our place in nature."

What business executive used to redistribute his wealth by walking down the streets in New York City?

John D. Rockefeller

Mr. Rockefeller was the role model of what other business executive who was motivated by serving humanity?

Bill Gates

Who was the first UNICEF Goodwill Ambassador?

The first was entertainer Danny Kaye, appointed in 1954, the same year that he appeared in the hit movie "White Christmas." UNICEF Ambassadors since then have included Peter Ustinov, Richard Attenborough, Audrey Hepburn, Youssou N'Dour, Johann Olav Koss, Vendela Kirsebom, George Weah, Jessica Lange, Roger Federer and Marco Antonio Solís.

Members of the British monarchy are well known for global humanitarian service. Which one is well remembered?

Princess Diana of Wales (1961-1997) was active in various charities seeking improvements in human welfare, from AIDS to a campaign to prevent landmines. She visited terminally ill people across the world and championed animal welfare programs. Other causes that Princess Diana supported included Help the Aged, the Trust for Sick Children, the youth branch of the British Red Cross, Chester Childbirth Appeal, National Hospital for Neurology and Neurosurgery, Dove House, Meningitis Trust, Welsh National Opera, Preschool Playgroups Association, Royal School for the Blind, Malcolm Sargent Cancer

Fund for Children, the Guinness Trust, Birthright, Variety Club, National Children's Orchestra, Royal Brompton Hospital and Eureka.

Chapter 25

QUOTES APPLICABLE
TO NON-PROFIT SERVICE

Acts of Kindness, Humanity

"Where there is charity and wisdom, there is neither fear nor ignorance."
— Francis of Assisi

"The life of a man consists not in seeing visions and in dreaming dreams, but in active charity and in willing service."
—Henry Wadsworth Longfellow

"I alone cannot change the world, but I can cast a stone across the waters to create many ripples. It's not how much we give but how much love we put into giving."
—Mother Teresa

"The value of a man resides in what he gives and not in what he is capable of receiving. It is every man's obligation to put back into the world at least the equivalent of what he takes out of it."
—Albert Einstein

"How wonderful it is that nobody needs to wait a single moment before starting to improve the world."
—Anne Frank

No act of kindness, no matter how small, is ever wasted."
—Aesop

"I can do things you cannot. You can do things I cannot. Together we can do great things."
—Mother Teresa

"Your life should be about finding the intersection of your greatest passion and the world's greatest needs."
—Gary White, founder of Water.org

"You are not here merely to make a living. You are here in order to enable the world to live more amply, with greater vision, with a finer spirit of hope and achievement. You are here to enrich the world, and you impoverish yourself if you forget the errand."
—Woodrow Wilson

"As we work to create light for others, we naturally light our own way."
—Mary Anne Radmacher

"No one is useless in this world who lightens the burdens of another."
— Charles Dickens

"You can't make footprints in the sands of time by sitting on your butt. And who wants to leave butt-prints in the sands of time?"
—Bob Moawad

"A few people of integrity can go a long way."
—Bill Kauth

"To ease another's heartache is to forget one's own."
—Abraham Lincoln

"Those who are happiest are those who do the most for others."
—Booker T. Washington

"Unless someone like you cares a whole awful lot, nothing is going to get better. It's not."
—Dr. Seuss

"And if everyone lit just one little candle, what a bright world it would be."
—Song

"The only people who can change the world are people who want to. And not everybody does."
—Hugh MacLeod

"Today I shall behave as if this is the day I will be remembered."
—Dr. Seuss

"And in the end, the love you take is equal to the love you make. All you need is love."
—Beatles

Value of Non-Profit Organizations

"The non-profit institution neither supplies goods or services. Its "product" is neither a pair of shoes nor an effective regulation. Its product is a changed human being. The non-profit institutions are human-change agents. Their "product" is a cured patient, a child that learns, a young man or woman grown into a self-respecting adult; a changed human life altogether."
—Peter Drucker

"Difficult things we do quickly. The impossible takes a little longer."
—David Ben-Gurion

"I don't know of any other organization that's raised more money than golf has, because if you are a baseball player, you're a football player, you're a hockey player, if you're just a businessman, and you want to raise some money for a charity, what do they do? They have a golf tournament. They have a golf outing, and they go out and they do it."
—Lee Trevino

Making a Difference

"I've always respected those who tried to change the world for the better, rather than just complain about it."
—Michael Bloomberg

"I resolved to stop accumulating and begin the infinitely more serious and difficult task of wise distribution. Wealth is not to feed our egos, but to feed the hungry and to help people help themselves."
—Andrew Carnegie

"If you want to change the world, be that change."
—Eliezer Jaffe

"Every man must decide whether he will walk in the creative light of altruism or the darkness of destructive selfishness. This is the judgment. Life's persistent and most urgent question is "What are you doing for others?"
—Martin Luther King Jr.

"The purpose of life is not to be happy. It is to be useful, to be honorable, to be compassionate, to have it make some difference that you have lived and lived well."
—Ralph Waldo Emerson

"Life's most persistent and urgent question is, what are you doing for others? Everyone can be great, because everyone can serve."
—Martin Luther King Jr.

"There is no exercise better for the heart than reaching down and lifting people up."
—John Holmes

"Service to others is the rent you pay for your room here on Earth."
— Muhammad Ali

Charity

"To give away money is an easy matter and in any man's power. But to decide to whom to give it and how large and when, and for what purpose and how, is neither in every man's power nor an easy matter."
—Aristotle

"Even the smallest person in the world can change the course of the universe."
—JRR Tolkien ("Lord of the Rings")

"We make a living by what we get. We make a life by what we give."
—Winston Churchill

"I would rather have it said, 'He lived usefully,' than, 'He died rich.'"
—Benjamin Franklin

"Helping people doesn't have to be an unsound financial strategy."
—Melinda Gates

"If a free society cannot help the many who are poor, it cannot save the few who are rich."
—John F. Kennedy

"Philanthropy is commendable, but it must not cause the philanthropist to overlook the circumstances of economic injustice which make philanthropy necessary."
—**Martin Luther King, Jr.**

"Think of giving not only as a duty but as a privilege. I was trained from the beginning to work, to save, and to give."
— **John D. Rockefeller**

"It's not just about being able to write a check. It's being able to touch somebody's life."
—**Oprah Winfrey**

"Give, but give until it hurts. It's not how much we give but how much love we put into giving."
—**Mother Teresa**

"Successful people are always looking for opportunities to help others. Unsuccessful people are always asking, "What's in it for me?""
—**Brian Tracy**

"When we give cheerfully and accept gratefully, everyone is blessed."
—**Maya Angelou**

"You have not lived today until you have done something for someone who can never repay you."
—**John Bunyan**

"That's what I consider true generosity: You give your all, and yet you always feel as if it costs you nothing."
—**Simone de Beauvoir**

"When we give cheerfully and accept gratefully, everyone is blessed."
—Maya Angelou

"The most treasured and sacred moments of our lives are those filled with the spirit of love. The greater the measure of our love, the greater is our joy. In the end, the development of such love is the true measure of success in life."
—Joseph Wirthlin

"If you're in the luckiest one percent of humanity, you owe it to the rest of humanity to think about the other 99 percent."
—Warren Buffett

"Charity is a supreme virtue, and the great channel through which the mercy of God is passed onto mankind."
—Conrad Hilton

""A bone to the dog is not charity. Charity is the bone shared with the dog, when you are just as hungry as the dog."
—Jack London

"Charity begins at home, but should not end there."
—Thomas Fuller

"Charity is injurious unless it helps the recipient to become independent of it."
—John D. Rockefeller

"We have the right as individuals to give away as much of our own money as we please in charity; but as members of Congress we have no right to appropriate a dollar of the public money."
—Davy Crockett

"If you haven't got any charity in your heart, you have the worst kind of heart trouble."

—Bob Hope

"Charity begins at home, and justice begins next door. There are not a few among the disciples of charity who require, in their vocation, scarcely less excitement than the votaries of pleasure in theirs."

—Charles Dickens

"Every good act is charity. A man's true wealth hereafter is the good that he does in this world to his fellows."

—Moliere

If we put our trust in the common sense of common men and 'with malice toward none and charity for all' go forward on the great adventure of making political, economic and social democracy a practical reality, we shall not fail."

—Henry A. Wallace

Community Service

"I slept and I dreamed that life is all joy. I woke and I saw that life is all service. I served and I saw that service is joy."

—Kahlil Gibran

"Citizen service is the very American idea that we meet our challenges not as isolated individuals but as members of a true community, with all of us working together. Our mission is nothing less than to spark a renewed sense of obligation, a new sense of duty, a new season of service."

—President Bill Clinton

"If you want to lift yourself up, lift up someone else."

—Booker T. Washington

"A community is like a ship; everyone ought to be prepared to take the helm."
—**Henrik Ibsen**, poet and playwright

Staying True to Purpose

"Compassion is an action word with no boundaries. A strong spirit transcends rules. The new pushes the old out of the way and retains what it wants to. Act your age, not your shoe size. There are no accidents, and if there are, it's up to us to look at them as something else, and bravery is what creates new flowers. Don't let your children watch television until they know how to read, or else all they'll know how to do is cuss, fight and breed. Despite everything, no one can dictate who you are to other people."

—**Prince**, music legend

Volunteerism

"The magnitude of our social problems will require that all citizens and institutions make a commitment to volunteering as a way of life and as a primary opportunity create needed change."

—**George Romney**, former Michigan governor

"How can we expect our children to know and experience the joy of giving unless we teach them that the greater pleasure in life lies in the art of giving rather than receiving."

—**James Cash Penny**

"Never doubt that a small group of thoughtful, committed citizens can change the world; indeed, it's the only thing that ever has."

—**Margaret Mead**, anthropologist

"Everyone can be great because anyone can serve. You don't have to have a college degree to serve. You don't even have to make your subject and your

verb agree to serve. You only need a heart full of grace and a soul generated by love."

—Dr. Martin Luther King, Jr.

"You cannot help someone get up a hill without getting closer to the top yourself."

—General Norman Schwarzkopf

"How wonderful it is that nobody need wait a single moment before starting to improve the world."

—Anne Frank, *Diary of a Young Girl*

"There is no better investment of time and money that in the life of a child. They are the future." —Alma Powell
"Seek to do good, and you will find that happiness will run after you."

—James Freeman Clarke

"No man can become rich without himself enriching others."

—Andrew Carnegie

"The moral test of a society is how that society treats those who are in the dawn of life- the children; those who are in the twilight of life- the elderly; and those who are in the shadow of life-the sick, the needy and the handicapped."

— Hubert Humphrey

"We can do no great things, only small things with great love. There is a tremendous strength that is growing in the world through sharing together, praying together, suffering together and working together." —Mother Theresa
"Volunteers are the only human beings on the face of the earth who reflect this nation's compassion, unselfish caring, patience, and just plain love for one another."

—Erma Bombeck

"The miracle is this — the more we share, the more we have."
—Leonard Nimoy

"It is one of the most beautiful compensations of this life that no man can sincerely try to help another without helping himself. You cannot do a kindness too soon, for you never know how soon it will be too late."
—Ralph Waldo Emerson

"Volunteering creates a national character in which the community and the nation take on a spirit of compassion, comradeship and confidence."
—Brian O'Connell

"Never before has man had such a great capacity to control his own environment, to end hunger, poverty and disease, to banish illiteracy and human misery. We have the power to make the best generation of mankind in the history of the world."
—President John F. Kennedy

"He has a right to criticize, who has a heart to help. To ease another's heartache is to forget one's own."
—Abraham Lincoln

"The best way to not feel hopeless is to get up and do something. Don't wait for good things to happen to you. If you go out and make some good things happen, you will fill the world with hope, you will fill yourself with hope."
—Barack Obama

"It is our collective and individual responsibility to protect and nurture the global family, to support its weaker members and to preserve and tend to the environment in which we all live. I believe that to meet the challenge of our times, human beings will have to develop a greater sense of universal responsibility. We must all learn to work not just for our own self, family, or nation but for the benefit of all humankind. Universal responsibility is the

key to human survival. It is the best foundation for world peace, the equitable use of natural resources, and through concern for future generations, the proper care of the environment."

—**The Dalai Lama**

"Older, younger, anyone can help. We've learned that our legislators listen, and people with passionate and thoughtful concerns make a difference every day. We've had constituents initiate legislation, lobby for it, organize meetings and events, and, of course, call, mail, e-mail and visit legislators to express their views. It's really great to see how much difference that individuals can make."

—**Doris Day**, singer-actress

"If I can stop one heart from breaking, I shall not live in vain. If I can ease one life the aching, or cool one pain, or help one fainting robin unto his nest again, I shall not live in vain."

—**Emily Dickinson**

"The greatest poverty that can afflict the human spirit is the loss of a generous heart. You will know that success has slipped away when your passion for helping others grows cold."

—**Bill Lane Doulos**

"The debt that each generation owes to the past, it must pay to the future."

—**Abigail Scott Dunaway**

"Volunteerism is the voice of the people put into action. These actions shape and mold the present into a future of which we can all be proud."

—**Helen Dyer**

"Keep on sowing your seed, for you never know which will grow. Perhaps it all will."

—**Ecclesiastes**

"A hundred times every day I remind myself that my inner and outer life depends on the labors of other men, living and dead, and that I must exert myself in order to give in the measure as I have received and am still receiving. Only a life lived for others is worth living."
—Albert Einstein

"It is one of the most beautiful compensations of this life that no man can sincerely try to help another without helping himself."
—Ralph Waldo Emerson

"Doing nothing for others is the undoing of ourselves."
—Benjamin Franklin

"I shall pass through this world but once. Any good therefore that I can do or any kindness that I can show to any human being, let me do it now. Let me not defer or neglect it, for I shall not pass this way again. The best way to find yourself, is to lose yourself in the service of others."
—Mahatma Gandhi

"If every American donated five hours a week, it would equal the labor of twenty million full-time volunteers. When you are kind to someone in trouble, you hope they'll remember and be kind to someone else. And it'll become like a wildfire."
—Whoopi Goldberg

"Help your sister's boat across the water, and yours too will reach the other side." Kindness can become its own motive. We are made kind by being kind."
—Eric Hoffer (1902-83)

"If you ever need a helping hand, it is at the end of your arm. As you get older you must remember you have a second hand. The first one is to help yourself. The second hand is to help others."
—Audrey Hepburn

"Whenever you are to do a thing, though it can never be known but to yourself, ask yourself how you would act were all the world looking at you and act accordingly. Every human being feels pleasure in doing good for another. May I never get too busy in my own affairs that I fail to respond to the needs of others with kindness and compassion."

—Thomas Jefferson

"We cannot close ourselves off to information and ignore the fact that millions of people are out there suffering. I honestly want to help. I don't believe I feel differently from other people. I think we all want justice and equality, a chance for a life with meaning. All of us would like to believe that if we were in a bad situation someone would help us."

—Angelina Jolie

"The unselfish effort to bring cheer to others will be the beginning of a happier life for ourselves."

—Helen Keller

"It is from the numberless diverse acts of courage and belief that human history is shaped. Each time a man stands up for an ideal or acts to improve the lot of others or strikes out against injustice, he sends forth a tiny ripple of hope, and crossing each other from a million different centers of energy and daring, those ripples build a current that can sweep down the mightiest walls of oppression and resistance."

—Robert F. Kennedy

Gratitude

"As we express our gratitude, we must never forget that the highest appreciation is not to utter words but to live by them. We must find time to stop and thank the people who make a difference in our lives."

—John F. Kennedy

"This a wonderful day. I've never seen this one before. Let gratitude be the pillow upon which you kneel to say your nightly prayer. And let faith be the bridge you build to overcome evil and welcome good. When we give cheerfully and accept gratefully, everyone is blessed."
—Maya Angelou

"Thankfulness is the beginning of gratitude. Gratitude is the completion of thankfulness. Thankfulness may consist merely of words. Gratitude is shown in acts."
—Henri Frederic Amiel

"Reflect upon your present blessings, of which every man has plenty; not on your past misfortunes, of which all men have some."
—Charles Dickens

"You cannot do a kindness too soon because you never know how soon it will be too late."
—Ralph Waldo Emerson

"They do not love, that do not show their love."
—William Shakespeare

"Never in the field of human conflict was so much owed by so many to so few."
—Winston Churchill

"The highest tribute to the dead is not grief but gratitude."
—Thornton Wilder

"When you are grateful, fear disappears and abundance appears."
—Anthony Robbins

"When I started counting my blessings, my whole life turned around."
— Willie Nelson

"Everyone can be great because anyone can serve. You don't have to have a college degree to serve. You don't even have to make your subject and verb agree to serve. You only need a heart full of grace and a soul generated by love."
—Dr. Martin Luther King, Jr.

"At times, our own light goes out and is rekindled by a spark from another person. Each of us has cause to think with deep gratitude of those who have lighted the flame within us. He who does not reflect his life back to God in gratitude does not know himself."
—Albert Schweitzer

Piglet noticed that even though he had a Very Small Heart, it could hold a rather large amount of Gratitude."
—A.A. Milne, "Winnie-the-Pooh"

"Enough is a feast."
—Buddhist proverb

"And in the end, the love you take is equal to the love you make."
—Beatles

"Got no checkbooks, got no banks. Still I'd like to express my thanks. I've got the sun in the morning and the moon at night."
—Irving Berlin

"Feeling gratitude and not expressing it is like wrapping a present and not giving it."
—William Arthur Ward

"When it comes to life the critical thing is whether you take things for granted or take them with gratitude. I would maintain that thanks are the highest form of thought; and that gratitude is happiness doubled by wonder."
— G.K. Chesterton

"Take full account of what excellence you possess, and in gratitude remember how you would hanker after them, if you had them not."
—Marcus Aurelius

"Be thankful for what you have; you'll end up having more. If you concentrate on what you don't have, you will never, ever have enough."
—Oprah Winfrey

"I think that real friendship always makes us feel such sweet gratitude, because the world almost always seems like a very hard desert, and the flowers that grow there seem to grow against such high odds."
—Stephen King

"Courtesies of a small and trivial character are the ones which strike deepest in the grateful and appreciating heart."
—Henry Clay

"Beth ceased to fear him from that moment, and sat there talking to him as cozily as if she had known him all her life, for love casts out fear, and gratitude can conquer pride."
—Louisa May Alcott

"Let us rise up and be thankful, for if we didn't learn a lot today, at least we learned a little, and if we didn't learn a little, at least we didn't get sick, and if we got sick, at least we didn't die; so, let us all be thankful."
—Buddha

"The way to develop the best that is in a person is by appreciation and encouragement."

—Charles Schwab

"He is a wise man who does not grieve for the things which he has not, but rejoices for those which he has."

—Epictetus

"The deepest craving of human nature is the need to be appreciated."

— William James

"Silent gratitude isn't very much to anyone."

—Gertrude Stein

"We should certainly count our blessings, but we should also make our blessings count."

—Neal A. Maxwell

Chapter 26

WHAT IT TAKES TO BE A LEGEND

Leadership Advice From the Halls of Fame

Do you admire people who went the distance? Have you celebrated organizations that succeeded? I hope that you are and will continue to be distinctive.

This essay is to give insights into those who leave legacies. The secret to long-term success lies in mapping out the vision and building a body of work that supports it. The art with which we build our careers and our legacy is a journey that benefits many others along the way.

These are the ingredients that make a legend:

- Significant business contributions.
- Mature confidence and informed judgment.
- Courage and leadership.
- High performance standards.
- Professional innovation.

- Public responsibility.
- Ethics and integrity.
- Cultural contributions.
- Giving to community and charity.
- Visionary abilities.
- Commitment to persons affected (stakeholders).

I have been blessed by receiving several Legend honors. What I remember the most are the ceremonies and the nuggets of wisdom that flowed. The commonality was the zest of giving back the honors to others.

The first was a Rising Star Award, presented to me in 1967 by Governor John Connally. That was the first time that I was called Visionary, and that experience told me to live up to the accolades later. The governor whispered to me, "Get used to wearing a tuxedo. Live up to the honor by saluting others."

That same year (1967), I met singers Sonny and Cher, little knowing that 26 years later, I would be inducted into the Rock N' Roll Hall of Fame and that they would hand me the award. I remarked to Sonny that I often quoted his song "The Beat Goes On" as analogous to change management, and he was pleased. Cher recalled the 1971 occasion where she and I visited at a jewelry store on Rodeo Drive in Beverly Hills, California. I remembered that we drank champagne in a pewter cup. Her quote: "There are new ways to approach familiar experiences," and I have applied that to corporate turnarounds.

It was by being inducted into the U.S. Business Hall of Fame that I met Peter Drucker. We subsequently worked together, doing corporate retreats. You'll note his endorsement on the back cover of my signature book, The Business Tree™.

One year, I received several awards. I got a Savvy Award, for the top three community leaders. I was a Dewar's profile subject. I had gotten a standing ovation at the United Nations for volunteer work that was my honor to do (especially since it enabled me to work with my favorite actress, Audrey Hepburn).

Subsequently, I was judging a community stewardship awards program. I quizzed, "Why is it that the same old names keep popping up? There are great people to honor other that those of us from business, high society or other top-of-the-mind awareness. What this community needs is an awards program that people like us cannot win."

I was then challenged to come up with such a program, the result being the Leadership in Action Awards. At the banquet, the swell of pride from the winning organizations was heartening to see. These unsung heroes were finally getting their just recognition for community work well done.

One cannot seek awards just for glorification reasons. However, recognition programs are a balanced scorecard that involves the scrutiny of the company and its leaders by credible outside sources.

Awards inspire companies of all sizes to work harder and try more creative things. Good deeds in the community are not done for the awards; they just represent good business. Receiving recognition after the fact for works that were attempted for right and noble reasons is the icing on the cake that employees need. Good people aspire to higher goals. Every business leader needs to be groomed as a community leader.

Recognition for a track record of contributions represents more than "tooting one's own horn." It is indicative of the kind of organizations with whom you are honored to do business. The more that one is recognized and honored, the harder that one works to keep the luster and its integrity shiny. Always reframe the recognition back to the customers, as a recommitment toward serving them better and further.

Characteristics of a Legend
- Understands that careers evolve.
- Prepares for change, rather than becoming the victim of it.
- Realizes there are no quick fixes in life and business.
- Finds a blend of perception and reality, with heavy emphasis upon substance.
- Has grown as a person and professional and quests for more enlightenment.
- Has succeeded and failed and has learned from both.
- Was a good "will be" in the early years, steadily blossoming.
- Knows that one's dues paying accelerates, rather than decreases.

Best Advice to Future Legends

Fascinate yourself with the things you are passionate about. Be fascinated that you can still be fascinated. Be glad for people who mentored you. Be grateful for the opportunities that you have had. Be proud of yourself and your accomplishments. Do not let the fire burn out of your soul.

There comes a point when the pieces fit together. One becomes fully actualized and is able to approach their life's Body of Work. That moment comes after years of trial and error, experiences, insights, successes and failures.

As one matures, survives, life becomes a giant reflection. We appreciate the journey because we understand it much better. We know where we've gone because we know the twists and turns in the road there. Nobody, including ourselves, could have predicted every curve along the way.

However, some basic tenets charted our course. To understand those tenets is to make full value out of the years ahead. The best is usually yet to come. Your output should be greater than the sum of your inputs.

This is accomplished by reviewing the lessons of life, their contexts, their significance, their accountabilities, their shortcomings and their path toward charting your future.

- Whatever measure you give will be the measure that you get back.
- There are no free lunches in life.
- The joy is in the journey, not in the final destination.
- The best destinations are not pre-determined in the beginning, but they evolve out of circumstances.
- You've got to give in order to get.
- Getting and having power are not the same thing.
- One cannot live entirely through work.
- One doesn't just work to live.
- As an integrated process of life skills, career has its place.
- A body of work doesn't just happen. It is the culmination of a thoughtful, dedicated process, carefully strategized from some point forward.

ABOUT THE AUTHOR

Hank Moore is an internationally known business advisor, speaker and author. He is a Big Picture strategist, with original, cutting-edge ideas for creating, implementing and sustaining corporate growth throughout every sector of the organization.

He is a Futurist and Corporate Strategist™, with four trademarked concepts of business, heralded for ways to remediate corporate damage, enhance productivity and facilitate better business.

Hank Moore is the highest level of business overview expert and is in that rarified circle of experts such as Peter Drucker, Tom Peters, Steven Covey, Peter Senge and W. Edwards Deming.

Hank Moore has presented Think Tanks for five U.S. Presidents. He has spoken at six Economic Summits. As a Corporate Strategist™, he speaks and advises companies about growth strategies, visioning, planning, executive-leadership development, futurism and the Big Picture issues affecting the business climate. He conducts independent performance reviews and Executive Think Tanks nationally, with the result being the companies' destinies being charted.

The Business Tree™ is his trademarked approach to growing, strengthening and evolving business, while mastering change. Business visionary Peter Drucker termed Hank Moore's Business Tree™ as the most original business model of the past 50 years.

Mr. Moore has provided senior level advising services for more than 5,000 client organizations (including 100 of the Fortune 500), companies in transition (startup, re-engineering, mergers, going public), public sector entities, professional associations and non-profit organizations. He has worked with all major industries over a 40-year career. He advises at the Executive Committee and board levels, providing Big Picture ideas.

He has overseen 400 strategic plans and corporate visioning processes. He has conducted 500+ performance reviews of organizations. He is a mentor to senior management. This scope of wisdom is utilized by CEOs and board members.

Types of speaking engagements which Hank Moore presents include:

- Conference opening Futurism keynote.
- Corporate planning retreats.
- Ethics and Corporate Responsibility speeches.
- University—college Commencement addresses.
- Business Think Tanks.
- International business conferences.
- Non-profit and public sector planning retreats.

In his speeches and in consulting, Hank Moore addresses aspects of business that only one who has overseen them for a living can address:

- Trends, challenges and opportunities for the future of business.
- Big Picture viewpoint.
- Creative idea generation.
- Ethics and corporate responsibility.
- Changing and refining corporate cultures.
- Strategic Planning.
- Marketplace repositioning.
- Community stewardship.
- Visioning.

- Crisis management and preparedness.
- Growth Strategies programs.
- Board of Directors development.
- Stakeholder accountability.
- Executive Think Tanks.
- Performance reviews.
- Non-profit consultation.
- Business trends that will affect the organization.
- Encouraging pockets of support and progress thus far.
- Inspiring attendees as to the importance of their public trust roles.
- Making pertinent recommendations on strategy development.

Additional materials may be found on Hank Moore's website: www. hankmoore.com

A free eBook edition is available with the purchase of this book.

To claim your free eBook edition:

1. Download the Shelfie app.
2. Write your name in upper case in the box.
3. Use the Shelfie app to submit a photo.
4. Download your eBook to any device.

A **free** eBook edition is available
with the purchase of this print book.

CLEARLY PRINT YOUR NAME ABOVE IN UPPER CASE

Instructions to claim your free eBook edition:
1. Download the Shelfie app for Android or iOS
2. Write your name in **UPPER CASE** above
3. Use the Shelfie app to submit a photo
4. Download your eBook to any device

Print & Digital Together Forever.

Snap a photo	Free eBook	Read anywhere

The Morgan James
Speakers Group

www.TheMorganJamesSpeakersGroup.com

We connect Morgan James published
authors with live and online events
and audiences whom will benefit
from their expertise.

CPSIA information can be obtained
at www.ICGtesting.com
Printed in the USA
LVHW102138170123
737379LV00020B/348